To maureen,
a guide line to 'Dutch people'
and their customs!

June 28, 2002.

# CULTURE SHOCK!
## Netherlands

Enjoy your
trip to Europe!

The
Groenenbergs.

Hunt Janin

D1176666

**Graphic Arts Center Publishing Company**
Portland, Oregon

**In the same series**

| | | | |
|---|---|---|---|
| Argentina | Egypt | Korea | Spain |
| Australia | Finland | Laos | Sri Lanka |
| Austria | France | Malaysia | Sweden |
| Bolivia | Germany | Mauritius | Switzerland |
| Borneo | Greece | Mexico | Syria |
| Britain | Hong Kong | Morocco | Taiwan |
| Burma | Hungary | Myanmar | Thailand |
| California | India | Nepal | Turkey |
| Canada | Indonesia | Netherlands | UAE |
| Chile | Iran | Norway | Ukraine |
| China | Ireland | Pakistan | USA |
| Cuba | Israel | Philippines | USA—The South |
| Czech Republic | Italy | Singapore | Venezuela |
| Denmark | Japan | South Africa | Vietnam |

Barcelona At Your Door
Chicago At Your Door
Havana At Your Door
Jakarta At Your Door
Kuala Lumpur, Malaysia
 At Your Door
London At Your Door
New York At Your Door

Paris At Your Door
Rome At Your Door
San Francisco At Your
 Door

A Globe-Trotter's Guide
A Parent's Guide
A Student's Guide

A Traveller's Medical
 Guide
A Wife's Guide
Living and Working
 Abroad
Working Holidays
 Abroad

Illustrations by TRIGG

© 1998 Times Editions Pte Ltd
© 2000 Times Media Private Limited
Reprinted 1998, 1999, 2000, 2001
Revised 2000

This book is published by special
arrangement with Times Media Private Limited
Times Centre, 1 New Industrial Road, Singapore 536196
International Standard Book Number 1-55868-400-X
Library of Congress Catalog Number 97-074476
Graphic Arts Center Publishing Company
P.O. Box 10306 • Portland, Oregon 97296-0306 • (503) 226-2402

Printed in Singapore

# CONTENTS

*In the Netherlands you are never very far from water.*

# PREFACE

In 1780 John Adams, who was then the American envoy to the *Staten-Generaal* (the States General, i.e. the Dutch parliament) and who later became the second President of the United States, wrote home to his wife:

> I am very much pleased with Holland. It is a singular country. It is like no other ... The frugality, industry, cleanliness, etc. here deserve the imitation of my countrymen.

Today, more than two centuries later, the Netherlands is still a singular country like no other. I hope that *Culture Shock! Netherlands* will give you a useful introduction to what has aptly been called the country of mild happiness.

This book would not have been possible without the help of many Dutch men, women and even children. I cannot thank all of them here but do want to acknowledge the excellent comments and suggestions made by Elsbeth and Rob Nieuwenhuijs of Noordwijk; Francine and Lucas de Booy of Naarden; Tjalling and Heleen Nuis of Middelburg; Inez Coppoolse at the Royal Netherlands Embassy in London; Carlo van Praag, Senior Researcher at the Social and Cultural Planning Office in Rijswijk; and Petronella van Gorkom of The Hague.

Every effort has been made to ensure that the information presented here is accurate. But conditions do change and I strongly urge anyone who is planning to visit, live or work in the Netherlands to check first with the nearest Netherlands Embassy or Consulate or with other competent Dutch authorities to get the latest word on rules and regulations.

The Netherlands has gone from strength to strength since this book was first published in 1988. This new edition is largely the work of Ria van Eil who has lived in both the Netherlands and abroad. The photographs appearing in this book were all taken by the author unless they are otherwise attributed.

# NETHERLANDS

WEST FRISIAN ISLANDS

Waddenzee

*NORTH*

*SEA*

Texel

Zuiderzee/IJsselmeer
Barrier Dam

GRONINGEN
Groningen

FRIESLAND

DRENTHE

Zuiderzee
(IJsselmeer)

NORTH
HOLLAND

Zaanstad

Haarlem
AMSTERDAM

North
Canal

FLEVOLAND

OVERIJSSEL

IJssel

Enschede

Loosdrecht
Lakes

Apeldoorn

Leiden

The Hague

Zoetermeer

UTRECHT
Utrecht

Amersfoort

GELDERLAND

Hook of Holland
Europoort

Nieuwe
Maas

SOUTH
HOLLAND

Lek

Arnhem

Waal

N

GERMANY

Rotterdam

Nijmegen

Dordrecht

Rhine R.

East Schelde

NORTH BRABANT

Breda

Tilburg

ZEELAND

West Schelde

Schelde

Eindhoven

Maas

LIMBURG

BELGIUM

Maastricht

6

# Chapter One

# A LAND OF SKY AND WATER

Vast uninterrupted skies, enormous cloudscapes, a soft ever-changing light, and everywhere you look, water – the North Sea, rivers, lakes, canals, locks, ponds and *slootjes* (narrow drainage ditches).

Even if you are not a landscape artist, you will still appreciate the quiet beauty of this well-ordered country. And when you spend some time there, you will also be favourably impressed by the very tall, prosperous and above all highly competent people who inhabit it.

The Netherlands is a small, very densely-populated country of about 16 million people located on the North Sea at the estuaries of several major rivers. It is often called "Holland" because in the 17th century the former province of Holland was economically and politically dominant. Officially, however, the country today is referred to as the Netherlands rather than Holland.

The term "Netherlands" is not only more accurate but also conveys an essential fact about the country. As the Dutch words *neder* (low) and *land* (country) suggest, it is indeed low-lying. Today about

27% of it is below sea level and if all the dikes and dunes were breached, much of the most densely populated part of the country would quickly be under water. The famous children's story about Hans Brinker, who plugged a leak in a dike with his finger until help could come, is less known in the Netherlands than in Britain or the US, probably because it is so far-fetched. As Han van der Horst rightly describes it in *The Low Sky*, when a dike does begin to give way "the water comes like a wall ... boring a deep hole in the ground immediately behind the dike. It then spreads out, thundering and boiling, sweeping away everything in its path – trees, cattle, people..."

## PLUSES AND MINUSES

The odds are that you will like the Netherlands. In contrast to the situation in many other countries, its rich culture is readily accessible to foreigners thanks to the linguistic capabilities of the Dutch themselves. As a result, your own stay in the Netherlands will probably be pleasant, interesting and relatively easy. There will be three good reasons for this:

- The Dutch have a long tradition of tolerance and they like foreign people, foreign ideas and foreign things.
- Because they are world traders and world travellers, they are very good with languages. Seventy-three percent of the Dutch speak a foreign language (usually English); 44% speak two (usually English and German); 12% speak three (usually English, German and French).
- The Dutch have created a very egalitarian, prosperous, caring society where institutions and technology work well and where there is little violent crime. The Netherlands is therefore a comfortable, efficient and safe place where expatriate families can live, work and travel without much difficulty.

8

Admirable as it may be, however, this society is not without some thorny problems:

- **Drugs and crime:** It is an offence to produce or traffic in both hard or soft drugs in the Netherlands. Drug use, however, is not an offense per se. Dutch policy aims to minimise the adverse impact of drugs by helping addicts rehabilitate. The Dutch believe that addicts are more likely to seek help if they do not have to fear being prosecuted or branded as criminals.

  The Netherlands is a relatively safe place to live as violent crimes are not very common. Petty crime, however, is rampant. Burglary, vandalism, theft and the like are thought to be chiefly the work of 'junks' (addicts of hard drugs). In the big cities, crime has risen on trains and buses too, with conductors being attacked by passengers with no ticket.

- **Immigrants and asylum seekers:** Some immigrants from Turkey and Morocco, and asylum seekers from many other countries, have had difficulty adjusting to urban life in the Netherlands and now form a distinct underclass. Many ethnic Dutch perceive them as responsible for more than their share of unemployment and premeditated (but usually nonviolent) crimes.

- **Congestion:** The Netherlands is nowhere near as densely populated as, say, Hong Kong or Singapore but nearly 16 million big people live in this little country. Having too many people for the space available results in a great number of rules and regulations (needed so that everyone's rights will be protected), a fair amount of pollution and traffic gridlock during rush hours. Another sign of congestion is that there are very few places in the Netherlands where you cannot hear an automobile going by.

## THE REASON FOR WRITING THIS BOOK

Such pluses and minuses, however, only reflect the fact that the Dutch have a unique culture which they value highly. They are usually more than willing to overlook social mistakes made by foreigners but the well-briefed foreigner should make fewer mistakes. And since the goal of *Culture Shock! Netherlands* is to help you become that well-briefed foreigner, let us begin with a quick lesson in Dutch geography.

# Chapter Two

# GETTING YOUR BEARINGS

The Netherlands is conveniently located on the western edge of the Eurasian land mass – on the North Sea and at the estuaries of the Rhine, the Maas and the Scheldt rivers. It is flanked by Belgium on the south and southwest and by Germany on the east. The United Kingdom is roughly 100 miles (160 km) to the west, on the other side of the shallow, choppy North Sea. Much appreciated by many Dutch travellers, *la douce France* ("sweet France") is about the same distance to the southwest, on the other side of Belgium.

## *A LANDSCAPE SHAPED BY HUMAN HANDS*

Nearly everything under the luminous Dutch skies is man-made and tailored to human measure. There are no Alps, Grand Canyons, Sahara Deserts or vast forests here. What you will find instead is a small scale but very charming tapestry, geometrically woven of carefully maintained cities, villages, canals, polders, lakes, roads, bridges, farm houses and meticulously cultivated fields.

Foreign visitors have always been favourably impressed by the Netherlands. An 18th century Italian historian commented on the cleanliness of the villages and the neatness of the countryside. In the same era, Sacheverall Stevens, an English gentleman, was enthusiastic about his own travels from Utrecht to Amsterdam "along one of the most agreeable roads in all Europe," which he said was like "an avenue in the best laid out garden." With the exception of some inner city districts, most of the Netherlands is still impeccably clean and neat today.

The population density of about 1,202 inhabitants per square mile (465 per sq km) is one of the highest in the world – about 20 times that of the US and twice that of the UK. This is due not so much to excessive numbers of people as to the small size of the country itself. The Netherlands is only 193 miles (310 km) long from north to south. Including such major bodies of water as the Waddenzee (*zee* means sea) off the province of Friesland and the freshwater IJsselmeer (*meer* means lake) between Friesland, Flevoland and North Holland, it has a total area of about 16,163 square miles (41,863 sq km) and is just a little bigger than nearby Belgium.

## HIGHS AND LOWS

The Dutch are the first to admit that most of the Netherlands is *zo plat als een pannenkoek* (as flat as a pancake). Compared with neighbouring countries, there is not much geographical diversity here. The highest point is Drielandenpunt in the southernmost tip of the country, where the German and Belgian frontiers meet. This boasts an elevation of 1,053 feet (321 m). There are also a few low hills, initially composed of debris left by glaciers which retreated a million years ago, in the Utrechtse Heuvelrug southeast of Utrecht and in the Veluwe west of Apeldoorn.

*Its flat countryside makes the Netherlands perfect for bicycle trips.*

At the opposite end of the spectrum, the lowest point in the Netherlands is near Rotterdam – at Nieuwerkerk aan de IJssel, more than 22 feet (-6.74 m) below sea level.

## REGIONS OF THE NETHERLANDS

### The West

A broad featureless plain in the western part of the country, originally composed of marine and river-borne clays, is now the most densely populated region. Known as the Randstad, it contains the four major cities of the Netherlands – Amsterdam, Rotterdam, The Hague and Utrecht – and is the home of six million people. The Randstad is at best only a few feet above sea level, so if all the dikes and dams broke most of it would soon be under water – as would Schiphol, the Netherlands' splendid international airport, which is more than 14 feet below sea level and was formerly part of the bed of Haarlem Lake.

13

## *The Southwest*

In the southwest, four big rivers (the Rhine, Maas, Waal and Scheldt) in the provinces of South Holland and Zeeland flow into the North Sea and have formed estuaries, islands and a wide, flat delta there. This area was especially vulnerable to flooding and is now the site of the huge Delta Works. In southern Limburg, the flat Dutch plains – now pleasant fertile landscapes highlighted by manor houses and old farms – give rise to the Ardennes hills of Belgium.

## *The North and the East*

The northern and eastern parts of the Netherlands border on Germany and are much more rural than the Randstad, although population and industrialization are increasing in this predominately agricultural area as well. But the pace of life here is still slower than it is in Amsterdam or Rotterdam and the inhabitants are not given to as many words.

The cultural attractions of these regions include some of the medieval commercial ports (such as Staveren and Kampen) of the Hanseatic League; scenic Giethoorn with its picturesque canals; and, south of Groningen, the *hunebeds* – prehistoric burial chambers which date from 2,000 B.C.

The northern province of Friesland offers truly excellent outdoor recreation. The best activity in summer is boating – sailing, cruising under power or simply rowing on the many lakes and rivers. Many Dutch people simply love the water and are excellent with all vessels, large or small. The boating in Friesland is so good, in fact, that I have moved my own classic English skiff, *Hope of Glory*, which was built on the River Thames and used there for 100 years, to the little Friesland village of Langweer.

The best outdoor activity in the winter is skating. On the rare occasions when a really cold winter freezes the canals hard enough, as it did in 1997, the famous *Elfstedentocht* (Eleven Towns Tour) is held. This begins in icy darkness at 5:30 a.m. and goes through 11

Frisian towns along a 123 mile (199 km)-long course. In 1997, 80 extra trains had to be laid on in the Netherlands to bring tens of thousands of spectators who came to watch 300 competitive skaters and more than 14,000 touring skaters tackle the course. The winner became, as always, a national hero.

## DUNES, DIKES, POLDERS AND CANALS

Hydraulic engineering, i.e., water management, is the single most important factor in shaping the Dutch landscape. Natural sand dunes along the coast have been planted with tough grasses to stabilize them. These play an essential role in protecting inland areas from high tides and are off-limits to hikers.

Where necessary, the dunes are backed up by dikes, which the Dutch have been making since 500 b.c. when the Frisians first piled up rudimentary mounds of dirt known as *terpen* and lived on them like castaway sailors. These early peoples must have had a very hard life (in A.D. 50 the Roman naturalist Pliny described them as a "wretched race") but by the year 1200 the Frisians were building the first true dikes and creating the first polders.

The Dutch came close to losing their war against the water in the 13th century when 35 big floods swept over low-lying areas, creating the Zuiderzee in 1287. But their brilliant response to this threat was the windmill, which could slowly but surely lift huge amounts of water and thus transform submerged or soggy areas into dry, productive polders – always good sites for farms, houses, cities and (much later) for factories and airports as well.

The first drainage windmill was built in the Netherlands in 1414. After the devastating St. Elizabeth's Day Flood of 1421 which is said to have killed 10,000 people and submerged 20 villages. Many more windmills were put into operation. In the 17th century and, helped by 43 windmills, the great hydraulic engineer Jan Adriaenszoon Leeghwater (appropriately enough, his surname means "empty water") created polders to the north of Amsterdam. A network of drainage

15

*Muskrats can seriously weaken dikes by burrowing into them. This muskrat trapper is employed by the Dutch government.*

canals, their water levels carefully regulated by windmills, crisscrossed the polders and kept the water at bay.

## CREATING LAND FROM WATER

The process of land reclamation picked up speed in the 19th and 20th centuries. Haarlem Lake was drained in four years, beginning in 1848, and after the floods of 1916 the Zuiderzee was transformed into the IJssel Lake by a barrier dam completed in 1932. To prevent a recurrence of the disastrous 1953 flood, the Delta Plan was drawn up. This ambitious project reached a dramatic point in 1986, when Queen Beatrix inaugurated a storm-surge barrier in the Eastern Scheldt. At extremely high tides, this huge dam, which is two miles long and based on two artificial islands, regulates in an environmentally sensitive way the flow of water in an estuary 5 1/2 miles wide and 115 feet deep.

Here is the Dutch success story in hydraulic engineering: since the 13th century the Dutch have managed to wrest from the water about 3,820 square miles (9,896 sq km) of dry land. Large-scale land reclamation, however, has now come to an end. The shallow Waddenzee in the north of the country could easily be drained but it is an important sanctuary for birds and seals. Given the very strong Dutch commitment to protecting the environment, there is very little chance that it will ever be reclaimed.

## THE CLIMATE OF THE NETHERLANDS

Located so close to the North Sea, the Netherlands has a cool maritime climate with the four seasons common to northern European lands. Damp, mild and sometimes foggy, it is rarely Arctic-cold – winter temperatures average only about 37° F (2.7° C) – but there is often a stiff wind and the windchill factor can make it seem much, much colder. Snowfalls are usually light and occur only on average 28 days per year. Frozen ponds (and sometimes the canals themselves) provide truly excellent skating.

*The windmill has helped transform the Dutch countryside and remains an internationally recognised symbol of the country.*

Summers are moderate and are ideal for sailing and other water sports, with temperatures averaging about 65° F (18° C). On an average day, three-fifths of the sky is clouded and there are only about 25 perfectly clear days each year, but on the remaining days, fantastic cloudscapes usually highlight the deep blue skies.

Alas, this is a damp climate and all days are not fair: the annual average rainfall of about 31 inches (790 millimetres) is distributed fairly evenly throughout the year, though it tends to be higher in autumn.

A Dutch lady once told me, "There is no such thing as bad weather. There is just bad clothing." This is a very good point. Officially, the climate of the Netherlands may be maritime and temperate but in practice it is also quite changeable. The well-prepared visitor will therefore bring warm, layered, windproof clothing for autumn and winter and will have rain gear and a sweater close at hand for the rest of the year.

# Chapter Three

# WHAT TO SEE AND WHEN TO SEE IT

Despite its small size, there are plenty of things to see and do in the Netherlands. Sports and entertainment will be discussed in the chapter on "Living in the Netherlands." What we will do here is to look at some of the best man-made and natural attractions the country has to offer.

## *MAN-MADE ATTRACTIONS*
Over the centuries the industrious Dutch have created many marvellous things. To reduce this embarrassment of riches to a manageable size, one has to be very selective. Here are some recommendations:
*   The major cities of the Randstad: Amsterdam, Rotterdam, The Hague and Utrecht.
*   Other attractive cities: Delft, Haarlem, Leiden (this is the Dutch spelling; "Leyden" is a British spelling) and Maastricht.

- Feats of hydraulic engineering: the Kinderdijk windmills, the Afsluitdijk (Barrier Dam) and the Delta Works.

- Examples of life at opposite ends of the social spectrum: the peat diggings in the province of Overijssel and the royal palace of the House of Orange, known as Het Loo.

## MAJOR CITIES OF THE RANDSTAD

If good things come in small packages, the Netherlands certainly qualifies. By world standards, the country's four major cities are really quite small. They are also very close together:

### Amsterdam

Most of the more than 750,000 inhabitants of Amsterdam would assert that their city is the pinnacle of trade, finance and culture in the Netherlands. Indisputably, it is the largest city as well as the capital – but it is not the seat of government, which is The Hague. Built on the banks of two rivers (the IJ and the Amstel), ringed with a network of old canals and dotted with splendid brick homes and world-class museums, Amsterdam is a glorious city. But like other European cities it has a seamier side as well – the well-known "coffee shops" which openly sell soft drugs, a great deal of petty crime (most of it drug-related) and an infamous red-light district, consisting of three or four streets where prostitutes openly display themselves behind red-lighted windows.

Amsterdam's beginnings were modest enough. In 1275 a Count of Holland accorded trading privileges to a little fishing village on the Amstel river built on a *dam* (dike). The city gradually grew up around this village centre, which became Amsterdam's main square, the Dam. In 1610 a central ring of new canals was dug and the Herengracht (the Lords' Canal; *gracht* means canal), the Keizersgracht (Emperor's Canal) and the Prinsengracht (Princes' Canal) – became highly desirable building sites for the mansions of newly-rich merchants.

It was in this era – the 17th century, now known as the Golden Age and discussed in the chapter on Dutch culture – that Amsterdam reached the apogee of its artistic and financial glory.

Rembrandt himself moved from Leiden to Amsterdam in 1630 and died there 39 years later. The Amsterdam stock exchange flourished: paper options on cargoes of spices and other goods shipped from the Netherlands East Indies (now Indonesia) were being actively traded and caused the same anxieties as the rise and fall of stocks still do more than 350 years later.

In fact, asked whether Dutch stocks would rise or fall, a Jewish merchant of Spanish origin gave an answer in 1688 which is still timely today. "The shares are shrouded in such a semi-divine haze," he wrote, "that the more one thinks about it, the less he understands; and the more shrewd he is, the more mistakes he makes!"

In any case, the best way to see Amsterdam now is to walk along the Herengracht and the other canals, admiring the 17th and 18th century homes with their striking gables and facades. Excellent maps and pamphlets and reliable advice can be obtained from the Netherlands' tourist information centre, abbreviated as VVV (Vereniging voor Vreemdelingenverkeer) and conveniently located opposite Amsterdam's central railway station.

There are 350 VVV centres in the Netherlands, all marked with three blue V's on a white triangle. They are staffed by competent, helpful people who can probably answer any question a visitor is likely to have. VVV centres can be found in all Dutch cities and in many towns as well.

Walks in Amsterdam can also be combined with the popular boat tours (Rondvaart), which ply the most important canals. Other not-to-be-missed sights include:

- The Jordaan, Amsterdam's most picturesque neighbourhood, with the photogenic warehouses, homes and quays of the Brouwersgracht (Brewers' Canal).

- The national art museum (Rijksmuseum), a stunning collection of Dutch art, including Rembrandt's celebrated painting of 1642, *The Night Watch*.

- The Vincent van Gogh National Museum (Rijksmuseum Vincent van Gogh), where many of his paintings and drawings can be seen.

- The red light district (Oudezijds Voorburgwal), where you can admire, as your taste dictates, either fine old houses along narrow canals or scantily-dressed ladies sitting invitingly behind curtainless windows.

- The Netherlands Maritime History Museum (Nederlands Scheepvaart Museum) in the city's port, where you can board the ship *Amsterdam*, a full-size (157 ft/48 m long), beautifully maintained replica of a Dutch East Indiaman of 1749 mounting 42 guns (cannon).

*Amsterdam is one of the most attractive cities in the world. As is the case in much of the country, water is a prominent feature.*

## *Rotterdam*

Located at the mouth of the Rhine, the Maas and their tributaries, Rotterdam (population 593,000) is the Netherlands' second largest city and the point where sea- and river-borne traffic meet and mingle. Originally it was only a small village on the *dam* (dike) of the river Rotte and had little to boast of until the great humanist Erasmus was born there in 1469. But in the late 16th and early 17th centuries, the Sea Beggars (Dutch fighters revolting against Spanish rule) built ports at Rotterdam for their own fleet and the city began to grow.

The city was captured by the French in 1794. Its prosperity went into a decline but its fortunes picked up again when Belgium and the Netherlands split up in 1830 and Rotterdam again became a transit point for river traffic. The 19th century witnessed a rapid development of the city and the port.

During World War II, Rotterdam was heavily bombed, first by the Germans in 1940 and then by the Allies in 1943. It was then sabotaged by the retreating Germans in 1944. But after the war, thanks to the industriousness of the Rotterdammers, the city arose from the ashes and is now the world's largest port in terms of tonnage handled, moving more than 314 million tons of cargo each year. If you like ships and quays, the best thing to do in Rotterdam is to take one of the SPIDO company's extremely interesting boat tours of this huge port.

## *The Hague*

Officially named 's-Gravenhage (literally, "the Count's hedge") but commonly known in Dutch as Den Haag and in English as The Hague (population 442,000), this pleasantly aristocratic and bureaucratic city is the seat of the Netherlands' government, its Parliament and a wide range of foreign embassies and missions. The Hague is also the seat of the International Court of Justice and the site of many international peace conferences.

Originally nothing more than a hunting lodge set in a dense forest, The Hague's rise began in about 1250 when the Count of Holland chose it as the site for a castle. A later Count moved his court there at the end of the 14th century. The Hague was pillaged by Dutch mercenaries in 1528 but in the 17th century it became the seat of the Dutch government and an important diplomatic centre.

In the 17th and 18th centuries, rich merchants built their mansions near the Binnenhof (its name means inner courtyard), the medieval heart of the city, and in the 19th century many Dutch colonial families returned from Indonesia to settle in The Hague. Queen Beatrix also chose to live in The Hague after her coronation in 1980. Royal Dutch Shell is headquartered here as well.

In the Binnenhof area are located the First Chamber of Parliament, which is similar to the British House of Lords or the US Senate; the Second Chamber, similar to the British House of Commons or the US House of Representatives; the Ministry of General Affairs; and part of the State Council. The Knights' Hall (Ridderzaal) dates from 1280. Each year the Queen, arriving in a golden coach, comes here to outline to the two Chambers the government's plans for the year.

*Located in The Hague, the Mauritshuis is one of the finest art museums in the world.*

25

Other worthwhile sights in The Hague are:

- The Royal Picture Gallery (Mauritshuis), one of the most beautiful classic buildings in the Netherlands, with fine paintings by Rubens, Rembrandt and Vermeer.

- The seaside resort of Scheveningen, which has a long sand beach well-suited to sunbathing and (for those who can endure the cold waters of the North Sea) swimming as well. There is also a casino and a long pier with a tall observation tower. Scheveningen's most attractive feature to me, however, is the nearby Oostduinpark (East Dune Park), where there is really excellent walking both along the beach itself and inland behind the big sand dunes protecting the coast.

## *Utrecht*

Still known for its university, which was established in 1636 and is now the largest in the Netherlands, Utrecht (population 233,000) is a crossroads for Dutch railways because it is located near the middle of the Netherlands. Every day 1600 trains pass through the city, making the town an important business and trade fair centre.

Utrecht was founded by the Romans in the first century A.D.; they called it Trajectum (ford), from which it gets its present name. A powerful bishopric was based here in medieval times with the blessing of the German emperors. The city is still the seat of Roman Catholicism in the Netherlands. Here, under the terms of the Union of Utrecht (1579), the seven northern provinces formed a united front against Spain. The Treaty of Utrecht (1713) curbed the imperial ambitions of France and ended the Spanish War of Succession. In the 19th century the city's old ramparts were replaced by parks and many new residential and commercial districts have sprung up since then.

Laced with bridges, the narrow Oudegracht (old canal) and Nieuwe Gracht (new canal) run through the centre of the city and are bordered by charming restaurants from which you can watch the passing boats. Rising 370 feet (122 m) into the air, the 14th century Dom Tower (Domtoren) is the tallest in the country and one of the most beautiful. St. Peter's Church (Pieterskerk), shaped like a cross, dates from 1048. The best collection of medieval art in the Netherlands is in Utrecht's Catharijneconvent Museum.

## OTHER ATTRACTIVE CITIES

### Delft

Dating from 1100, Delft (the name means moat) is the burial place of Prince William of Orange (1533-1584), whom the Dutch revere as the father of their country. Delft was also the home of Hugo de Groot (1583-1645), the father of international law who was better known as Grotius, and of the artist Johannes Vermeer (1632-1675). The blue-and-white earthenware known as Delftware, inspired by Chinese porcelain, has been famous since the 17th century and is still being made today.

This beautiful city should be seen on foot. A walk through Delft will reveal leafy canals, old churches, charming alleys and short streets, picturesque bridges and cool interiors suffused with a soft light from sky and water.

### Haarlem

The residence of the Counts of Holland, Haarlem was founded in the 10th century. The painter Frans Hals moved here in 1591. This city is now the heart of the tulip industry. Because storms on Haarlem Lake (the Haarlemmermeer) endangered Amsterdam and Leiden, the lake was drained in 1852. It became a productive settled region and, much later, the site of Schiphol airport. Local attractions include the Frans Hals Museum, the 15th century Great Church (Grote-of St. Bavokerk) and its adjacent Great Square (Grote Markt), and the 14th century Town Hall (Stadhuis).

## *Leiden*

Leiden is famous for its university, founded in 1575 and the first in the Netherlands. Rembrandt was a student there in 1620. This city is also remembered as a refuge for Protestants fearing persecution in their native countries.

In 1609 a group of Protestants known as the Puritans or Pilgrims moved from England, first to Amsterdam and later to Leiden. Eventually they decided to settle permanently in North America. So, after returning to England, they boarded the good ship *Mayflower* at the port of Plymouth and in 1620, upon reaching the coast of Cape Cod in what is now the state of Massachusetts, they set up Plymouth Colony, the first permanent settlement in New England.

There they governed themselves under a compact they had drawn up while still at sea. The great freedom they had experienced while in Amsterdam and Leiden found full expression in this "Mayflower Compact," which was the first constitution of the New World. Americans today still celebrate the Pilgrims' achievements on Thanksgiving Day.

Leiden's attractions now include a lovely old canal (Rapenburg) as well as the last windmill (Molen) built in the city in 1743 and used for milling grain. There are also five museums – highlighting respectively, ethnology, decorative arts, ancient civilizations, geology, scientific instruments and the Pilgrim Fathers.

## *Maastricht*

Founded by the Romans at the site where they bridged the river Maas, this city is a major industrial centre with a beautiful old section. St. Servatius' Basilica (St.-Servaasbasiliek) was built around 1000 on the site of a sanctuary then four centuries old. The Basilica of Our Lady (Onze Lieve Vrouwebasiliek) was already in place by 1000. The city's defensive walls (Walmuur) are highlighted by towers, trees and beautiful gardens.

Maastricht's most recent claim to fame is that it hosted a major European summit meeting in 1991 where leaders of the 12 European Union states signed a treaty calling for much closer monetary, commercial and political ties.

# FEATS OF HYDRAULIC ENGINEERING

## The Kinderdijk Windmills

Dutch windmills fall into two general categories: polder mills, designed to lift water, and industrial mills, which sawed timber, husked barley and processed the raw materials needed to grind wheat, make tobacco snuff, ropes, leather, spices and textiles. Windmills were the most powerful machinery of their day, not playthings, and could generate up to 100 horsepower. By varying the positions of their sails (blades), messages could also be sent. In fact, this was even done during World War II to signal British and American pilots flying over the Netherlands.

Because of their attractiveness, size and number, the 18 polder mills of Kinderdijk (Children's Dike) are well worth visiting. Dating from 1738, they were initially used to drain a marshy plain. They are now illuminated at night a week in September. One of these windmills (appropriately named De Blokker – a dedicated worker) is open to the public in the spring, summer and early autumn. In July and August, all 18 mills are set in motion each Saturday and sometimes other days as well.

## The Barrier Dam

Built between 1927 and 1932, the barrier dam (the Afsluitdijk) is 19 miles (30.5 km) long and 295 feet (nearly 90 m) wide at sea level. It tamed the Zuiderzee by transforming its southern half into a big lake now known as the IJsselmeer.

The most painless way to cross the Barrier Dam is of course by car but a more challenging way – and the best way to appreciate what the Dutch have accomplished here over such a vast stretch of turbulent water – is to ride a bicycle across it. A separate bike lane makes this safe to do at any time, but unless you have good gears and strong legs, a relatively windless day will prove best.

## The Delta Works

Two miles long and built on two man-made islands, the Eastern Scheldt Dam (Oosterscheldedam) is open to automobile traffic except when there are very high winds. A visit to Delta Expo, an exhibition centre on one of the islands, is well worthwhile. It offers not only graphic displays but also a boat trip showing how the Delta Works protect the southern part of the Netherlands from the tides and storms of the North Sea.

# LIFE AT OPPOSITE ENDS OF THE SOCIAL SPECTRUM

## The Peat Diggings of Overijssel

Part of the province of Overijssel is laced with small canals built for carrying peat and studded with shallow lakes formed when water flooded into the abandoned peat diggings. For example, the carefully restored and now postcard-perfect thatched-roof village of Giethoorn – named for the wild goat horns *(geitenhoorns)* once found there – owes its existence to the wet, cold, strenuous and badly-paid business of digging peat by hand in centuries past.

Today Giethoorn's reed-covered islands are still the source of the thick thatch for its homes and barns. These picturesque barns with their *kameeldak* (literally, camelroof, i.e., curved) roofs are accessible only by water – by flat-bottomed punts. The whole village is off-limits to cars but can easily be explored on foot or, even better, by renting a small boat – but preferably not at the height of the summer holiday season, when the charm of the village can be marred by swarms of visitors.

*A restored peat digger's house in the province of Overijssel. The long roof is to keep out the prevailing winds.*

## *The Royal Palace of Het Loo*

A keen sportsman, William III, the Prince of Orange, began work on Het Loo Palace (its name means "an open area in a forest") in 1685 as a hunting estate and a home for his court. Since then the palace has had a distinguished history in an elegant world far removed from that of the hoary-handed peat diggers.

Enlarged in 1692, Het Loo was captured by the French in 1795, was visited by Napoleon in 1811, became a summer residence for King William I in 1815 and was the home of Queen Wilhelmina after she abdicated in 1948. In 1969 Queen Juliana gave the palace to the nation and following extensive restoration work on the palace itself and its 1,626 acres of land and gardens, it was opened as a national museum (Rijksmuseum Paleis Het Loo) in 1984 – almost precisely 300 years after the first spade full of earth was turned for its construction.

Het Loo can be visited year-round but like many other outdoor sights in the Netherlands it will be at its best on a sunny summer day.

## NATURAL ATTRACTIONS

There is virtually nothing in this tiny country which has not been shaped in one way or another by human hands, so the word "natural" must be interpreted very loosely. With this caveat in mind, three natural attractions can be recommended: the De Hoge Veluwe National Park (which is also the site of the Kröller-Müller National Museum), the Wadden Islands and the bulbfields.

### De Hoge Veluwe National Park

Located between Apeldoorn and Arnhem, this 13,338 acre (5,500 hectare) park consists of beech, oak, pine and birch trees set off by heaths, sand dunes and lakes. It is home to hundreds of deer (red and roe), moufflon (wild sheep), wild boar, foxes, rabbits, badgers and many species of birds. The best time to look for some of these creatures is late afternoon in the winter and spring. From April to November, visitors can tour the park on the *witte fietsen* (white bicycles) provided free of charge.

This park is also the site of the Kröller-Müller National Museum, which houses paintings by van Gogh, Mondrian, French Impressionists and Dutch artists of the Golden Age. Contemporary sculpture is on display as well.

### Wadden Islands

Lying in an arc northwest of Friesland, the Wadden Islands have fine beaches of white sand, backed by high dunes. This is a very windy region which is most agreeable on sunny summer days. Texel, 15 miles long and 5 1/2 miles wide, is the biggest island and has three nature reserves.

Since driving cars is not permitted on some of the islands, bicycling and walking are the best ways to get around. The Waddenzee is so shallow that at low tide it can actually be crossed on foot – but this unique Dutch sport of *wadlopen* (mud-walking) can only be undertaken with a guide and never in winter.

Low tide uncovers vast areas of mud or sand *(wadden)* which are ideal feeding grounds for resident gulls and ducks. Many migratory birds feed and winter here, too, while seals bask on the sand banks off the North Sea coasts of the islands.

## *The Bulbfields*

Introduced from Turkey at the end of the 16th century, tulips have been grown with great success in the fields between Haarlem and Leiden.

The "great tulip mania" occurred in the 1630s when these flowers were in such demand throughout northern Europe that the Dutch threw their normal caution to the wind and feverishly began buying and selling bulbs purely on a speculative basis. Prices soared: at a time when a skilled worker was earning only 2.8 guilders a week, the rarest bulbs were changing hands at 6,000 guilders each.

The inevitable crash came in 1637 and provoked endless moralizing about the evils of speculation, which was denounced as undermining the proper Calvinist relationship between hard work and a good income.

Today the bulbfields cover more than 54,000 acres and produce 80% of the world's production –about 10 billion bulbs each year. These are best seen in all their glory in the spring – from mid-April until the end of May. This floral checker-board of vibrant colours can seen by car, train, even from an plane taking off or landing in the Netherlands or from the windmill at the Keukenhof (the National Flower Exhibition), where every year six million tulips, daffodils and hyacinths are planted across its nearly 80 acres.

# Chapter Four

# HOW DO THE DUTCH SEE THEMSELVES?

By drawing on some of the points made by the Royal Tropical Institute in Amsterdam when it teaches foreigners about life in the Netherlands and which are echoed by Han van der Horst in his excellent book *The Low Sky*, one can say that the well-educated Dutch like to imagine themselves as – and certainly hope that foreigners will see them as – an egalitarian, practical, well-organized people who value privacy and self-control, who are thrifty and drive a hard bargain, and who are experts in international trade.

## *THE DUTCH ARE NOT PERFECT*

To some extent, of course, this very flattering self-image is only a myth. In reality, the Dutch are certainly not angels. Their proverbial bluntness is not to everyone's taste. Many of them are neither intelligent, well-educated, tolerant, considerate, prosperous, multilingual, friendly towards foreigners nor low-key and quiet. Some of them, in fact, especially the hooligans at football (soccer) matches, fall very far short of the idealized national standards. Indeed, in 1997 one person died as a result of injuries sustained at a fight between rival clubs of football supporters.

Another shortcoming is that the Dutch are so committed to equality, compromise and avoiding conflict that they have created a labyrinth of rules and regulations from which there is no easy exit. Mastering all these sometimes conflicting legal and procedural requirements is hard enough for the Dutch themselves. And foreigners trying to make their way through this Kafkaesque maze may well begin to despair if they hear too often from Dutch bureaucrats the blunt statement, "That is not possible!"

What we are saying here is that the Netherlands is not, in fact, an earthly paradise. Despite your very best efforts, you may find that you simply cannot get along with some Dutch people. Nevertheless, the positive traits listed above are the ones set by the upper middle class and the ones which most Dutch try to teach their children at home and at school. So let us look briefly at each of these idealized national characteristics in turn.

## *THE DUTCH ARE EGALITARIAN*

The rich/poor gap which is so painfully visible in Britain, the US and in many other developed countries simply does not exist to the same extent in the Netherlands, which prides itself on being a truly egalitarian society. Indeed, since the end of World War II the Dutch have virtually eliminated life-threatening poverty in their own country. Thanks to a booming economy, the Netherlands' 2.6% unemployment rate is the lowest in the European Union.

Officially, only a small percentage of the people – mainly the unemployed, students and single-parent families – fall below the poverty line, which is set relatively high. This figure is deceptive, however, because the most likely reason these people are officially classified as "poor" is that for one reason or another they are not using

35

all the unemployment, housing and other social benefits to which they are fully entitled. In point of fact, it is estimated that only about 0.05% of all Dutch households are really in serious financial trouble.

One reason for this is that it is very difficult indeed for a person to fall through the tightly-woven safety net provided by the Dutch welfare system. Unless you are, say, a drug addict or a mentally ill person with no fixed address and who categorically refuses to ask for help, the government will give you various kinds of help and enough money to ensure your survival, albeit at a very modest level.

At the same time, however, it is equally difficult in the Netherlands to rise to the very top of the business world or any of the professions. Stiff and progressively higher taxes are only part of the problem. The real issue is that just as they do not like to see some people falling by the wayside, the Dutch do not like to see others rising too high: they really do practice social equality.

One proof of this is that there are said to be comparatively few "real" millionaires in the country—because it has been inflation and dot.com investments that have generated the wealth of most of the 200,000 people nominally in the millionaire category.

Perhaps a reflection of this fact is a classic Dutch saying *Doe maar gewoon, dan doe je al gek genoeg* – Behave normally, that's mad enough. The Dutch commitment to normality reflects a conviction that in such a small densely populated country, assertive, aggressive or flamboyant behaviour is inherently unequal. It is also likely to offend other people.

By the same token, riches should not be flaunted. Well-heeled individuals should not throw money around or treat themselves to lavish houses, expensive parties or flashy cars. And unlike the British monarchy, the House of Orange (the Dutch royal family) – aided, to be sure, by the Netherlands' rigorous privacy laws which keep the media at arms' length – maintains a low public profile, avoids scandals and shuns extravagances.

It is not surprising, then, that tolerance, moderation and respect for others are three cardinal virtues for the well-educated Dutch. These

Golden Rules not only encourage social equality in the society as a whole but also help ensure that the individual can pursue his or her own interests without any interference. The individual is considered to be the best judge of his or her destiny. A Dutch motto along these lines is *Laat iedereen in zijn waarde* – to each his own.

At the same time, the Dutch want equality for other people, too, both those who live in the Netherlands itself and those who are sunk into Third World poverty or who find themselves in war zones.

Simon Schama, the British historian who wrote the magisterial book *The Embarrassment of Riches* (1987), begins it with a quote from John Calvin, the puritanical theologian who was one of the leaders of the Protestant Reformation: "Let those who have abundance remember that they are surrounded with thorns, and let them take great care not to be pricked by them." Calvin apparently feared that prosperous Dutch citizens would become so morally tainted by their own wealth that they would selfishly refuse to care for the needy.

Perhaps it is with Calvin's stern warning embedded in their subconscious that the educated Dutch of today are so willing to help the less fortunate. There is an extensive social welfare system at home and widespread public support for generous foreign aid and for international peacekeeping operations abroad. Calvin would certainly approve: he would have no trouble defending these activities – chiefly on moral grounds, to be sure, but perhaps also as a practical way to keep the have-nots from becoming a threat to those who have a comfortable abundance.

## *THE DUTCH ARE PRACTICAL*

Most of the Dutch are less concerned with metaphysical questions than with finding practical solutions to immediate problems, the chief of which, on a national basis, has always been the war against the water. In this endless battle the Dutch, armed first with windmills and later with pumping stations, have been largely successful – "God made the world," runs the old saying, "but the Dutch made the Netherlands."

Eternal vigilance, however, is the price of this victory. The Dutch will literally never be able to drop their guard. Every day, the 1,200 miles of dikes, dams and dunes must be kept in good repair; every day, water which percolates into the polders (land reclaimed from the sea) must be drained and pumped out. No one has described the need for this vigilance better than the poet Hendrik Marsman (1899-1945):

> *en in alle gewesten* – And in every region
> *wordt de stem van het water* – The voice of the water
> *met zijn eeuwige rampen* – Telling of endless disaster
> *gevreesd en gehoord.* – Is heard and feared.

These prophetic words were borne out in 1953, when a very high tide driven by a very strong wind flooded 642,200 acres of the Netherlands, killing 1,865 people, making hundreds of thousands of others homeless and drowning more than a million cattle. The Dutch response – practicality here on a truly vast scale – was to build a network of huge dams (the Delta Works) to protect the southwestern coast and its inland areas.

Perhaps it is this practical, no-nonsense approach to water management which gives the Dutch some of their less adorable characteristics. To be sure, they can be helpful and friendly but they can also painfully direct, outspoken, stubborn and blunt – as implied by the term "Dutch uncle," i.e., a well-meaning but, when the occasion calls for it, an unrelenting critic.

In *The Embarrassment of Riches*, Simon Schama gives a 17th century example of Dutch straightforwardness. When the Dutch presented to Henry, Prince of Wales, a massive gold casket full of valuable annuity bonds, an English courtier tried to downplay the value of the present by dismissing it with the laconic sigh of *"puf."* The Dutch emissary quickly corrected him: *"Non puf est,"* he said in blunt Latin, *"sed aurum purum."* (This is not *puf*, but pure gold!)

Dutch self-assurance has continued down the years. Trying to explain the Dutch mentality to the US troops serving in the Netherlands during World War II, the American anthropologist Margaret Mead joked that "The Dutch are always right." Then, with tongue firmly in cheek, she added: "In this they resemble the Americans."

If some of the Dutch are very practical and think they are always right, it follows that they should also be good debaters. And indeed many of them are. These men and women are willing to offer their own opinions on any subject under discussion. *Ja, maar ...* (yes, but ...) is a common interjection whenever one speaker pauses for breath, however briefly, during a conversation.

And since they think they know how matters really should be arranged, some of the Dutch are also prone to grumble about the perceived injustices – personal, social, academic, job-related, national or international – which are allegedly being inflicted upon them every day. Even here, however, many Dutch manage to keep a sense of humour and do not take themselves too seriously. A Dutchman now in his seventies, for example, recalls that when he was growing up his father always told him: "Skip the complaints!"

## THE DUTCH ARE WELL-ORGANIZED

Because they like to lead busy lives, being on time is usually very important to the Dutch. Making – and keeping – appointments is no less important to them; to make sure they do, diaries are in frequent use, especially when the vitally important issue of *overleg* is involved.

### Overleg: The Search for Common Ground

*Overleg* has no exact equivalent in English. A literal translation would be "to consult together" but the British phrase "in conference" is more to the point.

*Overleg* is a slow, consensus-building exercise in which everyone at a meeting has the opportunity to participate. Teamwork is important here. The goal is not to rubber-stamp the chairperson's own preference for Solution A but to exchange information and to hammer out a workable compromise which all the participants can endorse.

Reaching a decision by this process can be time-consuming, but the Dutch believe that things move faster in the long run if the chairperson can announce with pleasure, *de klokken zijn gelijk gezet* – the clocks are all showing the same time, i.e. we are all agreed on Solution B.

One thing that really keeps even the non-religious Dutch on their toes is the Calvinist doctrine of hard work. A job must be done on time but equally important, it must also be done well. Shoddy work or corruption are not tolerated. Individuals or companies which do not maintain high standards will soon be out of business.

This is the reason visitors to the Netherlands are invariably impressed by the very high quality of Dutch products and by the visible pride which even small tradespeople (butchers, fishmongers, florists and cobblers) take in doing their job well. Perhaps this is because the non-religious Dutch of today are still aware of the traditional clergyman's *vermanende vinger* (wagging finger), warning them of the moral dangers of idleness and slovenly work.

*A high standard of living and an egalitarian ideal characterize Dutch society.*

## THE DUTCH VALUE PRIVACY AND SELF-CONTROL

Although they may not be as restrained and as polite as the British, the Dutch usually respect other people's privacy and would be the first to agree that a man's home is his castle. But the neighbours' home is their castle, too, and adults are supposed to exercise some self-control. To be sure, as we have indicated, not all Dutch are quiet, sober citizens and not all of them dislike gossip. But while it may be honoured in the breach, the cultural ideal is nevertheless to be considerate, not to cause commotion.

## GEZELLIGHEID: THE PURSUIT OF COSINESS

Within their immaculately clean homes (proudly exposed to public view because the curtains are rarely drawn), the Dutch can revel in *gezelligheid*, a national trait which defies easy translation into English. According to the dictionary, it means "cosiness" but this does not convey the full flavour of the term.

Rodney Bolt, a foreign writer living in Amsterdam, puts it very well in a *Xenophobe's Guide to the Dutch*. For him, *gezelligheid* is partly a sort of cosiness and partly a living-togetherness; the mood in a neighbourhood cafe on a cold winter's afternoon is *gezellig*; a mother will call "Keep it *gezellig!*" if she hears her offspring becoming dangerously boisterous. To this one can only add that gezelligheid is one of the prime ingredients in the recipe for the "mild happiness" which is so important to the Dutch.

## THE DUTCH ARE THRIFTY AND STRIKE A HARD BARGAIN

Despite their wealth, the Dutch have a long reputation as penny-pinchers. In his famous 18th century satire, for example, the French writer Voltaire tells us, tongue in cheek, that after his fictional hero Candide had been robbed in Suriname by a Dutch merchant, Candide complained, loudly and at length, to a Dutch judge – who patiently agreed to look into the matter when the merchant returned but in the meantime charged Candide 10,000 piasters for making too much noise and an additional 10,000 piasters for the hearing itself!

## THE DUTCH ARE EXPERTS IN INTERNATIONAL TRADE

Long before the Dutch East India Company was founded in 1602, Dutch seamen and merchants were deeply involved in international trade. Their descendants are now at the forefront of the current drive toward globalization, i.e., treating the whole world as a single unified market for goods, services and ideas.

Not for nothing is the Netherlands known as "the gateway to Europe." Nearly 5200 km (3,000 miles) of navigable inland waterways link the Netherlands to neighbouring Belgium, France and Germany. Forty percent of the road transport in Europe is handled by the Dutch. Schiphol, the Netherlands' main airport, has 80 airlines serving 220 destinations and handles more than 36 million passengers a year.

Rotterdam, strategically located at the mouth of the Rhine and the Maas, is a key transhipment point for foreign goods coming into northern Europe. Indeed, in terms of the tonnage handled, this is the busiest port in the world, where over 32,000 seagoing ships bring in nearly 314 million metric tons of cargo each year. A good part of this cargo is off-loaded onto smaller vessels which deliver goods to German buyers via the Rhine.

## A SUMMING UP

Even if you have never lived abroad before, you will probably find that living and working in the Netherlands is not particularly difficult. It bears repeating that the Dutch are not angels. But to get along with most of them all you really have to do, in a nutshell, is to follow the advice offered to the author by a young Dutch couple: "Be yourself," they said, "and respect other people."

*— Chapter Five —*

# A QUICK LOOK AT DUTCH HISTORY

The Netherlands is a very small country but its history is long and complex. Any summary of it must be highly selective and will probably appal professional historians. But as a newcomer you really cannot hope to understand the Netherlands of today unless you have at least a faint idea about the Netherlands of the past.

To make this task easier, let us see if we can find a common thread which will help make sense of a history which stretches back at least to 30,000 B.C. At the risk of great oversimplification, we can say that although Dutch history prior to the reign of Philip the Good (1396-1467) may not have a single unifying theme, later on we can indeed detect one, namely: the gradual movement toward greater national and personal freedom.

This movement toward more freedom still continues today. In fact it has always been an inspiration to other peoples, too: as Benjamin Franklin, the 18th century American statesman and inventor, put it, "In love of liberty and in the defense of it, Holland has been our example."

## *PREHISTORY*

The first faint traces of human settlement in the Netherlands date from about 30,000 B.C. By 9,000 B.C., Stone Age hunters and fisherman equipped with flint tools were eking out a precarious existence in what is now the Netherlands.

The first human settlements date from 5,300 B.C., when farmers and cattle herders settled in the south near Limburg. In the north of the country, men and women, known from their pottery as the Funnelneck Beaker people, buried their dead in massive rock tombs called *hunebeds*. Weapons and tools were made of bronze by 2,100 B.C. and of iron by 700 B.C. Farmers settled along the North Sea coast on artificial mounds *(terpen)* built to keep their settlements above the flood waters.

## *THE ROMANS*

Julius Caesar began subjugating the Celtic and Germanic tribes of the area in 57 B.C. Roman roads built along raised river banks were the next dikes and Roman forts later became the towns of Maastricht and Nijmegen. But in the third century A.D. Roman power began to ebb. After the legions were withdrawn, Angles and Saxons settled in the north and east of the Netherlands, mixing with the local Frisians.

## *MEROVINGIANS, CAROLINGIANS AND VIKINGS*

The Franks, a Germanic people, became the dominant group in the early Middle Ages. The most successful Merovingian king, Clovis (466-511), conquered all of Gaul (France). In 695 the Pope appointed the Anglo-Saxon missionary Willibrord to be archbishop of the Frisians and bishop of Utrecht, but Christianity spread only slowly in the northern Netherlands.

The Merovingians were overthrown by Pepin III, who established the Carolingian dynasty, named after his famous son, Charlemagne, who succeeded him in 768. Charlemagne reigned for 47 years and expanded his realm to such an extent that he was crowned in Rome as the Holy Roman Emperor. The social structure gradually changed as feudalism began to bind lords to their king, who gave them land in return for their military and financial support. These lords in turn granted land to their own vassals, who lived on the labour of the bondsmen (peasants) who were tied to the soil and who tilled the fields.

Vikings, those fierce sea-roving Norsemen, repeatedly plundered the Netherlands in the 9th and 10th centuries. On eight different occasions, for example, they destroyed the great trading centre in Dorestad (rebuilt in the 15th century, it is now known as Wijk bij Duurstede.) The Vikings could not be kept at bay until town and coastal defenses were strengthened in the 11th century.

## *A FRAGMENTATION OF POWER*

Between the 11th to the 14th centuries, the Netherlands consisted of numerous semi-independent principalities governed by counts. The name "Holland" dates from a deed of 1083. Over the years the county of Holland was extended at the expense of its neighbours. Trade increased, towns grew and the lot of the peasants improved as marshlands were reclaimed and new farming methods were introduced. Water boards were established to maintain the dikes and sluices.

## *BURGUNDIANS AND HABSBURGS*

The dukes of Burgundy gained control over parts of the Netherlands, Belgium and eastern France. After coming to power in 1419, Philip the Good set up assemblies (known as "states") consisting of representatives from the nobility, clergy and towns. In 1464, delegates from all the states met in Bruges (now in Belgium) – an event which can be considered a milestone on the road to freedom because it was the first meeting of what later became the States General, i.e., the Dutch parliament.

In the meantime, Burgundian lands prospered: Antwerp became the principal port, the cloth industry provided widespread employment and great artists (Jan van Eyck and Hieronymus Bosch) flourished. When Charles the Bold died, the duchy of Burgundy reverted to France and the other lands passed to the princely German house of the Habsburgs.

Another step toward political freedom came in 1477, when the States General forced Mary of Burgundy to sign the Great Privilege, a constitutional document conferring far-reaching local powers. The States General were entitled to meet whenever they liked and Mary was not permitted to wage war without their approval.

## *THE SPANISH NETHERLANDS*

The Emperor Charles V (1500-1558) ruled over a vast empire which embraced the Burgundian lands, the Spanish kingdoms of Aragon and Castille (including Mexico, Peru and the Philippines) and the Austrian States. He strongly opposed the Reformation but in 1555 was forced to sign a peace treaty which confirmed the right of German princes to choose freely either the Protestant or the Catholic religion for their subjects.

In practice, this meant that the Netherlands would remain Catholic but the Reformation was already so advanced there that magistrates refused to convict heretics and the repressive efforts of the Habsburgs failed. Charles abdicated in 1555 in favour of his son Philip II, who became king of Spain and lord of the 17 provinces then making up the Netherlands.

## *THE DUTCH REVOLT*

Philip fiercely resisted the growth of Protestantism and any decentralization of his royal government, thus offending William of Orange and the other great nobles who encouraged these liberal trends. At the same time, the economy took a sharp downturn, which added to the growing political unrest. In 1566, hundreds of noblemen petitioned the regent of the Netherlands (Margaret of Parma, Philip's half-sister) asking that the anti-heresy laws of the Inquisition be changed. One of Margaret's ministers, however, dismissed the nobles as "nothing but beggars" – an insult which led all those who opposed the Spanish government to proudly adopt the title of "Beggars" *(geuzen* in Dutch).

Philip sent in troops to crush Dutch opposition to his autocratic rule. William of Orange and thousands of other patriots fled from the Netherlands. Some of these exiles whose property had been seized by Philip's forces called themselves "Sea Beggars" *(Watergeuzen)* and took to the North Sea to oppose the Spanish. In 1572, the Sea Beggars and their allies captured Den Briel, a small seaport town. This success marked the beginning of a widespread popular uprising against Spanish domination.

In 1579, representatives from the seven northern (and predominantly Protestant) provinces signed the Union of Utrecht, under which they agreed to unite against Spain, maintain their traditional rights and liberties and allow freedom of religion. This agreement became the bedrock on which the freedoms of the Dutch Republic were founded.

## *A REPUBLIC IS BORN AND THE GOLDEN AGE BEGINS*

The States General assumed sovereign power in 1588, creating the Republic of the Seven United Provinces. Spain tried, but failed, to reconquer the northern Netherlands and under the terms of the Twelve Years' Truce of 1609, it gave de facto recognition to the Republic as an independent state.

The 17th century is known as the Golden Age because it was a time of remarkable cultural and economic progress in the Netherlands. Painting, architecture, music and other arts will be mentioned in the chapter on Dutch culture. The very fine achievements in these cultural fields, however, were made possible by the fact that during the early decades of the 17th century the two Dutch provinces of Holland and Zeeland became, with Amsterdam as their hub, the centre of Europe's trade with the rest of the world.

Grain, salt, wine, herring, textiles and spices were shipped to the Baltic states. Dealing in spices, Dutch merchants began the colonization of what is now Indonesia. The Dutch East India Company (also known by its Dutch initials as the VOC) was founded in 1602 and given control of the Netherlands' lucrative trade with Asia via the Indian ocean. For two centuries it was the biggest and most powerful trading organization in the world. Until it was eclipsed in the 18th century by the British East India Company, the VOC earned great profits: at one point, dividends on its shares ran as high as 3,600%.

As a result, shipbuilding and related industries (sail- and rope-making) flourished: by 1650 the Dutch had over 2,500 merchant ships and 2,000 fishing vessels. Sugar refining and cloth weaving provided additional profits and employment as well.

## EXPANSION ABROAD

Dutch maritime skills played a decisive role in the creation of a far-flung commercial and colonial empire during the 17th century.

In 1609, Henry Hudson, an English seaman then working for the Dutch East India Company, bought Manhattan (New York) from the local American Indians for a string of beads. Dutch traders occupied the Guiana coast (Suriname) in 1613. Three years later a Dutch ship rounded Cape Horn, off the tip of South America. Java (Indonesia) was colonized in 1619.

The Dutch West India Company, which traded with both Africa and the Americas, was founded in 1621. Nieuw Amsterdam (now New York) was settled in 1625. The Dutch West India Company took over Curaçao in 1634 and a Dutch governor general controlled the Antilles. Two years later there was also a Dutch governor general in Brazil.

Malacca (in Malaysia) was captured from the Portuguese in 1641. The Dutch discovered Tasmania and New Zealand the next year and Australia in 1644 but did not settle in any of these lands. They founded Cape Colony (South Africa) in 1652 and, finally, they occupied Ceylon (Sri Lanka) in 1658.

Dutch colonial possessions proved to be transitory, however, and today only the Netherlands Antilles (which consists of the islands of Aruba, Curaçao and Bonaire off Venezuela's coast, and Saba, St. Eustatius and southern St. Martin in the Leeward Islands) still belong to the Netherlands.

*Photo: Netherlands National Maritime Museum, Amsterdam*

*The Dutch East Indiaman,* Amsterdam *– a reminder of Dutch maritime history.*

## WARS WITH ENGLAND AND FRANCE

Fearing the Netherlands' near-monopoly in seaborne trade in the 17th and 18th centuries, however, England tried to claim hegemony over the North Sea. The clash between the mercantile policies of these countries led to four Anglo-Dutch wars between 1652 and 1780.

In the process, Louis XIV of France attacked the Netherlands in 1672 and although the country remained intact under the Peace of Nijmegen, the French invaded again in 1795 and were more successful. Napoleon Bonaparte set up his brother Louis as King of Holland and by 1813 this kingdom had formally become part of the French empire.

## A REUNITED COUNTRY AND THE REDUCTION OF ROYAL POWER

After Napoleon was defeated at Waterloo in 1815, Prince William I of Orange, the son of the last *Stadhouder* (the head of state) of the Republic of the Seven United Provinces, became King of the Netherlands, uniting the 17 northern and southern provinces after a separation of over 200 years.

William is remembered as the "merchant-king" because of the great economic progress which marked his reign. His political skills, however, were less pronounced. In 1830 the Brussels Revolution led to the independence of Belgium and in 1840 he abdicated after announcing his intention to marry a Roman Catholic countess.

A constitutional revision of 1848 had sharply curtailed royal power but a later King, William III, found it hard to accept these limitations. He clashed repeatedly with the parliament but in the end was soundly defeated and had to accept that henceforth Dutch rulers would be only the symbols of the unity of the Dutch people, rather than wielding any political power themselves. Constitutional monarchy was here to stay.

## *EVOLVING INTO AN INDUSTRIAL SOCIETY*

Between 1840 and the outbreak of World War I in 1914, the Netherlands gradually changed from an agricultural society to a modern market driven economy with a fair degree of government involvement. Machines took over much of the heavy manual work but brought in their wake many of the negative aspects of the Industrial Revolution, including child labour. Protests against these abuses grew, however, and a bill introduced in parliament in 1874 led to a government investigation into the condition of workers in factories.

As a result of the problems of industrialization and the controversies over religious education, political parties came into being around 1880. In 1887 the constitution was revised to extend the vote to more men. Women, however, did not get the vote until 1919.

Although at one point over 30% of the labour force was out of work during the Great Depression of the 1930s, the abundant raw materials from the Dutch East Indies and the Netherlands' strong position in international trade led to the growth of big multinational corporations such as Royal Dutch Shell and Philips.

# Chapter Six

# MODERN TIMES

Since the end of World War II in 1945 the Netherlands has experienced a great many changes. With growing prosperity has come an extensive social welfare network. "Pillarization," a unique way of organizing Dutch social life, has gradually disappeared. The Netherlands has become a multiracial society. Protecting the environment is now a major concern of government and citizens alike.

## WORLD WAR II AND ITS AFTERMATH

The Netherlands had been neutral during World War I and pacifist ideals remained very strong thereafter. But Germany invaded the Netherlands in 1940 and quickly overwhelmed the weak Dutch defenses. Queen Wilhelmina and her government found refuge in England, where through Radio Orange broadcasts she encouraged her people to resist the Germans.

Between 102,000-107,000 Jews were rounded up in the Netherlands and killed by the Nazis. One of these was a 13-year-old girl named Anne Frank, whose sensitive diary remains a masterpiece of this tragic era.

In 1944, Allied armies landed in Normandy and began the liberation of Europe. But the northern part of the Netherlands still had to suffer through a winter of famine, when starving people were reduced to eating tulip bulbs, before the whole country was finally set free in 1945 and the huge task of reconstruction could begin.

Understandably, during and after the war many Dutch were strongly anti-German, a feeling which has persisted to some extent to this very day, more than 50 years later, especially among the older generation. Here is a classic Dutch joke: when a Dutchman sees a German, he says to himself "I want my bike back!" This refers to the fact that during the war Germans soldiers often confiscated Dutch bicycles for their own use. In fact, more than 100,000 bicycles were confiscated in 1942 alone.

## FAR-REACHING CHANGES

With the war's end, important domestic and international changes came thick and fast in the Netherlands. To list but a few of them: Queen Wilhelmina was succeeded by her daughter Juliana in 1948. The foundations for an ambitious social welfare network were laid as the Dutch economy made steady progress. The former colony of Indonesia became independent. In 1949 the Netherlands joined the North Atlantic Treaty Organization (NATO) and in 1957 the Dutch were among the founders of the European Economic Community – now known as the European Union (EU).

### Prosperity and Social Services

In the 1960s, the Dutch economy continued to grow rapidly, aided by the discovery of huge natural gas reserves in the northeastern province of Groningen. These gas revenues helped finance a welfare state which, despite its well-publicized complexity and its many shortcomings, is still quite remarkable for the excellence, depth and breadth of its social services.

Although they put a very high value on these services and would not want to live without them, the Dutch themselves are quick to complain, however, that the welfare state as a whole is an impenetrable thicket of laws and regulations. You have to be a real expert to be able to make your way through it.

## *"Pillarization" Fades Away and Youth Flourishes*

General prosperity and wider educational opportunities also eroded the unique Dutch custom of *"pillarization"* (social compartmentalization), which we will discuss in the chapter on Dutch culture. New and more broadly-based political parties appeared, such as the Christian Democratic Appeal which embraced all the major religious factions.

In the same era, the youth subculture which had first appeared in California in the early 1960s quickly spread to the Netherlands. By 1965, Amsterdam's Provo (from *provocation*) movement was taunting Dutch authorities and infuriating the complacent Dutch middle class. The 1968 student revolt in Paris encouraged Dutch students to put forward demands of their own. Universities in the Netherlands gradually adapted themselves to most student demands and student activism declined in the 1970s.

## *A Multiracial Society*

Labour shortages prompted the Dutch to recruit large numbers of workers from foreign countries, including Turkey and Morocco, many of whom brought their families to the Netherlands in the 1970s and settled there permanently. Together with immigrants coming from Suriname and the Antilles in the 1980s and asylum seekers fleeing from upheavals in their native lands, these men, women and children have changed the Netherlands into a multiracial society.

More than 17% of the population of the Netherlands is now of non-Dutch origin. Since these newcomers want to preserve their own cultures, the task of fully assimilating them into Dutch culture has proved to be much more difficult than originally expected. Because of the importance of this issue to the ethnic Dutch, we will look at immigrants in greater detail in the last chapter, "Prospects for the Future."

## *PROTECTING THE ENVIRONMENT*

Queen Juliana was succeeded by her daughter Beatrix in 1980 and during the first decade and a half of her reign the Netherlands moved ahead on a wide variety of fronts. One of the most important of these was the growth of a strong environmental ethic – a commitment to protect the environment, not only in the Netherlands itself but also abroad.

Perhaps as an antidote to their very densely populated and highly developed society, the Dutch have always had a strong commitment to protecting the environment. A superb public transportation network (trains, trams and buses), highlighted by special low-cost tickets for commuters and students, has been created to wean people away from the use of city-choking automobiles.

Apartment dwellers seek a bit of "country life" by growing their own vegetables in carefully tended allotment gardens. The government's own Forestry Commission (Staatsbosbeheer) carefully manages the forests and woodlands in its charge. These are open to the public and are studded with trails, picnic areas and bike paths. More than 200 nature reserves managed by the privately-funded Nature Conservation Society (Vereniging tot Behoud van Natuurmonumenten) protect habitats for birds and other wildlife. Most of these are open to the public, too.

By the 1980s, however, the Netherlands was facing some very severe environmental problems. Its flat topography and low elevation encouraged the infiltration of salt water into farmlands. Big European rivers (the Rhine, Maas and Scheldt) carried toxic waste products through the country and deposited them in the North Sea. Industrialization, high population densities and intensive land use in the Netherlands itself exacerbated almost all kinds of pollution.

There was also a uniquely Dutch problem: disposing of all the manure produced each day by the country's 5 million cows and 14 million pigs – only a small portion of which could be used as fertilizer for farms.

These problems still persist but good progress is being made in dealing with them. The Dutch public and the Dutch government are deadly serious about cleaning up the environment and are demanding costly remedial efforts by industries and private citizens alike.

Dutch industries have drawn up more than 75 voluntary covenants with the government to reduce pollution and conserve energy. A new "Environmental Technology Valley" has been established in Apeldoorn to attract companies making innovations in environmental

*The Dutch work hard to protect the environment: a nature reserve in the central Netherlands.*

technology. Households are producing less waste and separate waste containers enable the waste to be collected and processed more efficiently. Commuters are encouraged to use bicycles, trains and buses rather than cars. Farmers are induced to cut back on the use of pesticides and artificial fertilizers.

In essence, a new balance is being struck between economic development on the one hand, and the conservation of nature on the other. A successful compromise along these lines was the Eastern Scheldt Dam, completed in 1986.

If necessary, the gates of the dam can be closed at high water levels to prevent floods. The daily tidal flows however, are not affected, thus assuring that the Eastern Scheldt remains a biologically productive waterway – and this was what the environmentalists and oyster farmers wanted.

## *International Cooperation*

Abroad, the Netherlands continues to play a very active role in international efforts to protect the global environment. For many years, to take just one example, the Dutch have worked closely with other countries along the Rhine and with Belgium to reduce trans-border river pollution.

# Chapter Seven

# A GENTLE SOCIETY: THE NETHERLANDS TODAY

What can we say about the Netherlands today – about the quality of life, social welfare, the economy, trade unions, domestic politics, military forces, Water Control Boards, foreign policies and, last but not least, about drugs and crime?

## *THE QUALITY OF LIFE IS VERY HIGH*

One of the things that may strike you after you have lived in the Netherlands for a few months is that the overall quality of life there is extraordinarily high.

The Dutch, too, think it is very high and would probably attribute this to a combination of factors: an excellent educational system, first-class health care, general prosperity, social equality, racial and religious tolerance, very little political extremism, very little real poverty, no slums, little violent crime, and a good balance (thanks to many rules and regulations) between the needs of the individual and the needs of society as a whole.

Allied to all this is, one can add, a long tradition of hard, competent work. Other countries may also have a saying along the lines of "Work before pleasure" but the Dutch give this adage a more humorous and more explicit twist: *werk gaat voor het meisje*, they say – "Work comes before the girlfriend!"

## GOOD MARKS FROM FOREIGN BUSINESSMEN AND OFFICIALS

This exceptionally high quality of life allows foreign businessmen to give the Netherlands good marks in all of the areas they consider to be priorities for employees being assigned there: accommodation, personal security, schooling for children, leisure facilities, environment (clean air and water), and cultural and social facilities.

In fact, according to a 1996 United Nations (UN) Human Development Report, which measured human progress by linking economic growth to social factors rather than looking at economic growth alone, the Netherlands is the best country to live in within the European Union and the fourth-best globally (after Canada, the US and Japan). A compelling case can be made, however, for the proposition that for the average man or woman in the street, the overall quality of life in the Netherlands is actually much higher than it is in the US or Canada.

Dutch life expectancy (an average of 78.1 years) is quite high and thanks to its enrolment rates in primary, secondary and tertiary schools, the Netherlands also scores well in educational achievement. Income distribution is above-average compared to other highly developed countries. Though the rate of violent urban crime has risen in the Netherlands, it is still low when compared with other developed countries (notably the United States).

## MILD HAPPINESS DESPITE SOME SHORTCOMINGS

But the UN report does not give the country a straight-A report card. As the Dutch press has noted, although the Netherlands clearly ranks among the world's top five industrialized countries in terms of living conditions, life expectancy, education levels and social investment, it scores below-average when it comes to spending for higher education and for the economic empowerment of women.

Still, according to official surveys by the Netherlands' central bureau of statistics, nine out of ten Dutch people say they are happy. As the Duke de Baena commented more than 30 years ago after his long service as a Spanish diplomat in the Netherlands, this is truly *le pays du petit bonheur* (the country of mild happiness).

The author's own informal surveys, randomly conducted in city streets, railway stations, bars and in the homes of Dutch friends, certainly confirm this: remarkably few Dutch citizens have anything negative to say (beyond complaining about the weather or the fact their country is so densely populated) when asked politely, "What do you think is *wrong* with your country?"

Most foreigners, too, like living in the Netherlands. As a Canadian professor working at the Free University of Amsterdam explained with a nice turn of phrase, "There's no undercurrent of violence here. When I go back to the US, people ask me what it's like in the Netherlands. I always tell them it's a gentle society. That's the word that really sums it up for me: gentle."

## SOCIAL WELFARE: THE SAFETY NET

Since the end of World War II the Dutch have created a far-reaching and very generous social welfare system, largely financed by revenues from natural gas. While quite complex and vulnerable to abuses, this system includes, among other things, unemployment benefits, housing allowances, child support, paid sick leave, income support, old age benefits and insurance for health care. There is, in short, a virtually unbreakable social welfare safety net designed to catch people before they fall into utter destitution.

There are four national insurance programmes and four employee insurance schemes. Buttressing this system are other important social services, for example, the General Family Allowance Act (this helps families support their children up to the age of 18) and the National Assistance Act (which helps those with no or minimal income).

The total cost of all these programmes is now so high that benefits must be administered more tightly if the country is to afford them. One immediate result has been that people who had not been working because of spurious physical or mental ailments have now had to go back to work, either full-time or part-time, if they cannot prove they are genuinely ill.

Nevertheless, as a general rule any person who has previously worked in the Netherlands but is now involuntarily unemployed will be supported at public expense – although possibly at a low level – while he or she is looking for another job.

## *A HEALTHY ECONOMY*

A highly-industrialized country which also has a strong agricultural sector, the Netherlands is preeminently a trading nation and plays a central role in the economic life of Western Europe. (See the chapter on "Doing Business in the Netherlands" for more details.)

At the same time, it is also a "post-industrial era" power because about 75% of its work force is employed in the service sector. Economic growth has been very strong in recent years. It was 3.7% in 1999 and was forecast to reach 4% in 2000. Unemployment has hit historic lows and there is work for every willing worker. Many of these new jobs – both full time and "flexi-work" – are held by women.

On the industrial front, three of the world's biggest multinational corporations are located here – Royal Dutch Shell, Unilever and Philips. Manufacturing employs about 23% of the labour force (the

*A Dutch dairy farm: agriculture still plays an important role in the economy.*

metal industry is the largest employer here); food, beverage and tobacco manufacturing enterprises rank second in terms of employment but first in production value. The petroleum products, chemical and electrical/electronics industries are also important: BP, Exxon and Texaco, among others, have major refineries or petrochemical plants in the Netherlands.

Intensive agriculture, especially dairy farming and horticulture, is another success story. The highly-mechanized agriculture sector employs just 4% of the work force but produces large surpluses for domestic food processing and for export. The Netherlands ranks third worldwide (after the United States and France) in agricultural export value. The milk yield per cow is among the highest in the world; much of it is processed into butter, cheese or condensed milk and exported. Huge numbers of pigs, calves and chickens are raised in sheds to produce meat and eggs. Hothouse vegetables and flowers are grown under acres of glass, while other vegetables, fruits, flowers, plants and bulbs are produced outdoors in meticulously-cultivated fields. Every

63

day the world's biggest flower auction (in Aalsmeer), which covers an area equal to 75 football fields, ships 18 million cut flowers and 2 million potted plants around the globe.

Given the Netherlands' geographical location, it is natural that for many centuries international trade has been a key component of the economy. Indeed, the value of Dutch imports and exports hovers at around 50 to 60% of the gross domestic product (GDP), a proportion far greater than that of the US or UK. Much of the Netherlands' trade is with Europe and North America. About 78% of Dutch exports go to the EU; most imports come in from Germany, followed by those from the EU and the US.

The Netherlands is thus a gateway for the flow of goods between Western Europe and the rest of the world. These arrive at well-equipped Dutch harbours: Europoort, the port area between Rotterdam and the North Sea, can accommodate the deepest-draft ocean-going ships, while Rotterdam itself handles more tonnage than any other port in the world. Goods continue on their final destinations by river boat, train, truck or petroleum pipeline.

## *MODERATE TRADE UNIONS*

As "social partners" working together with management and government, Dutch trade unions negotiate conditions of work, salary increases and holidays. Although the unions are still influential, their days of greatest power are probably now behind them. They feel they have an important stake in the existing economic order and in recent years they have held wage demands to moderate levels – on the premise that it is better to let economic growth lead to more jobs tomorrow rather than more pay today. The outcome is that there are very few strikes in the Netherlands.

Union membership rose more or less steadily from the end of World War II until the worldwide recession precipitated by the oil crisis of 1973. Since then, however, the internationalization of financial markets and of trade itself have strengthened management's hand and weakened labour's. Only 29% of Dutch workers now belong to unions, in contrast to about 67% in Belgium and 43% in the UK.

## *THE POLITICS OF ACCOMMODATION*

The Netherlands is a parliamentary democracy under a constitutional monarch, Queen Beatrix of the House of Orange-Nassau. In general, this political system works extremely well. Politicians are respected and trusted, more often than not; the Queen herself and the rest of the royal family are universally popular.

Since none of the many political parties can get a clear majority, coalition governments, based on the principles of tolerance and consensus, are the rule. In an electoral landslide in 1994, for example, the Christian Democrats – a religiously-based centrist party which had played an active role in the Dutch government for the past 75 years – were soundly defeated. There is now a ruling "Purple Coalition" between right and left wing parties, so named because it represents a compromise between the views of different political parties represented by the electoral colours red and blue.

Under the constitution as revised in 1848, Government ministers are accountable to an elected parliament rather than to the monarch. This legislative body, known as the *Staten-Generaal* (States-General), has two houses. The First Chamber (75 members) is elected by the municipal councils of the Netherlands' 12 provinces, known as the Provincial States. The Second Chamber (150 members) is directly elected; with as little as 0.66% of the total vote, a very small party or political movement can win a seat here.

Both houses share power with the government and control its policies. But since the views of all players in the political arena must be accommodated, a consensus is necessary. In many ways this is a good thing, but in practice much legislation undergoes so many amendments and refinements while it is being drafted that, as a Dutch newspaper complained, "a law designed to achieve a perfectly commendable goal thus quickly becomes an impenetrable tangle of clauses and sub-clauses."

The 672 municipalities *(gemeenten)* are important institutions of local government and are now getting the freedom to manage their own affairs. Presided over by a *burgemeester* (mayor), they are led by a directly elected council of from 7 to 45 members. Local standards for law and order are usually set by a "policy triangle" consisting of a mayor, a public prosecutor and a chief of police.

Flexibility is the hallmark here: the police, for example, are usually instructed to ignore the sale or use of soft drugs and to focus instead on more serious criminal offences. This is a classic example of the traditional Dutch policy of *gedogen*, a word which literally means "to tolerate." It is a policy under which certain offences which are punishable by law are not, in practice, prosecuted. Good examples are euthanasia and the use of soft drugs.

## MILITARY FORCES: SMALL BUT EFFECTIVE

National defence is provided by the Netherlands' small but well-trained and extremely well-equipped professional military forces, which participate frequently in NATO exercises and play an active role in the UN's international peacekeeping operations.

Conscription in the Netherlands ended in 1996. About 53,000 men and women now work in the Dutch armed forces, divided as follows: Royal Netherlands Army (23,500 people), the Navy (13,100), the Air Force (11,400), and the Marechaussee (4,600). The Marechaussee is a military police force which controls the country's borders and airports and guards the royal palaces.

## WATER CONTROL BOARDS

One of the oldest and historically most important democratic institutions in the Netherlands is the local Water Control Board. These Boards have the crucial task of protecting the land from flooding. They are also responsible for irrigation, drainage and water purification projects and for maintaining the canals and rivers. The senior officers of the Boards used to be appointed by the Crown, but are now publicly elected.

## *FOREIGN POLICY: NEUTRALITY, REALISM AND IDEALISM*

As a trading nation, the Netherlands was committed to a strict neutrality and was able to maintain its position during World War I. It tried to pursue the same policy when World War II broke out but the German invasion in 1940 made this impossible. After the war, the security threat posed by the Soviet Union prompted the Netherlands to put neutrality aside and to join NATO. It is now a member of many other international organizations, including the UN, the EU, the Organization for Economic Cooperation and Development (OECD), the Western European Union and the Council of Europe.

Because the Dutch have a very strong commitment to helping those less fortunate than themselves, "development cooperation" (i.e., foreign aid) is an integral part of Dutch foreign policy. The Netherlands provides assistance and expertise to many developing countries and was the second country (after Sweden) to achieve the internationally agreed aim of giving at least 0.7% of its Gross National Product (GNP) in this process.

## *DRUGS: SOFT AND HARD*

A "coffee shop" is a café where soft drugs are sold, subject to certain restrictions: no hard drugs may be sold; drugs may not be advertised; the "coffee shop" must not disturb the peace; no drugs may be sold to persons under 18; and no minors are allowed on the premises. The number of "coffee shops" has recently been reduced. The Dutch tolerate limited sales of soft drugs for personal consumption because, they explain, this lets the police concentrate on suppressing trafficking and consumption of hard drugs, e.g., heroin and cocaine, and keeps soft drug users outside the criminal circuit.

But in response to domestic and international criticism of these permissive drug policies (the French have denounced the Netherlands as "a drug state" and as "a paradise for drug tourists"), the Dutch government decided in 1996 to reduce from 30 to 5 grammes per customer the amount of soft drugs which can legally be sold in the "coffee shops" of Amsterdam and other cities. The number of coffee shops in Amsterdam, which had increased so rapidly in the 1980s (from 9 in 1980 to 101 in 1988), has now declined as well.

## Hard Drugs

It bears repeating here that in the big Dutch cities there is a good deal of petty, opportunistic theft. Much of this is related to the use of hard drugs: addicts (the Dutch refer to them as *junks*) steal things which they can sell quickly in order to buy the drugs they need to stave off the agonies of withdrawal.

Despite all the criticism they have received, the Dutch remain convinced their policy of paying less attention to soft drugs and more to suppressing hard drugs is paying off handsomely. The proof of the pudding, they might say, is that the number of *junks* per 1,000 inhabitants is significantly lower in the Netherlands (which has 1.6 addicts per 1,000 people) than it is in most other European countries (where the average is 2.7 addicts per 1,000). Deaths by overdose are lower than in other countries. In 1995, for example, the death rate from drug abuse was 2.4 people per million in the Netherlands, 9.5 per million in France, 20 per million in Germany, 23.5 per million in Sweden, and 27.1 million in Spain.

## SOME GOOD NEWS ON THE CRIME FRONT

Shoplifting and pocket-picking are the most common urban crimes. But new or expensive bicycles are also certain to disappear unless carefully secured with heavy-duty locks. Householders also take pains to make sure they have secure locks on all their doors. In Amsterdam, parked cars are broken into so frequently and their radios stolen so often that some cars display notices informing potential thieves that "There is no radio in this car."

There are two bits of good news on the crime front, however. Most importantly, as we have said, violent crimes are not common. Though they have increased over the last 10 years, they account for only a small percentage of the total crimes. This means that the Netherlands remains one of the least violent countries in the whole world.

Petty crime is still commonplace but is not likely to grow explosively for two reasons: law-abiding persons have become more careful and now have better security measures, and the number of young males (the demographic group most likely to commit crimes) has been declining.

The bottom line is that you will probably not be murdered or mugged in the Netherlands and that if you keep a close watch on your bicycle, car radio (just be careful where you park) and other worldly goods they are not likely to disappear.

# Chapter Eight

# THE CYCLE OF LIFE IN THE NETHERLANDS

In the cycle of life – childhood, student days, marriage, divorce, middle age, retirement, old age and death – there is often a special "Dutch touch" to these familiar human milestones. Knowing something about this will make it easier for you to understand and adjust to Dutch society.

## *NON-WORKING MOTHERS*

Compared to the US, UK and many other developed countries, there are still relatively few mothers working full-time in the Netherlands. In fact, only 25% of Dutch women think that having children and a career can be successfully combined.

There seem to be four reasons there are so many stay-at-home mothers:

- Certainly the most important is the very strong Dutch tradition of a familial society – a society where family life is extremely important and where the mother's constant presence in the house is seen as essential for the proper upbringing of the children.

- Homemakers themselves have always been valued highly. In the past, working mothers were accepted but not necessarily praised – indeed, they might even have been quietly criticized for being "overambitious." Self-esteem is not a problem here: non-working mothers today are every bit as self-confident as women who work.

- Dutch school children almost always come home for lunch, which the mother herself has to prepare. Children also come home from school at 3:30 p.m. or even earlier. The Netherlands lags far behind many other countries in providing child care facilities for 3-4 year olds: a nanny or any other kind of child care is costly and hard to find.

- There is sometimes no economic necessity for a woman to work because her husband's income may be adequate for family needs.

So, until very recently, it was expected as a matter of course that even well-educated, highly-trained young women would stop working when their first child was born and would not go back to full-time work until after the last child had left the nest. If they worked outside the home before then, it would be only at part-time jobs. Even today, 75% of the Dutch women who have children and who are also working are holding down part-time jobs.

## *Some Consequences*

Taking such a long break from full-time work in order to raise children means that Dutch women tend to fall behind their men in terms of work experience and the technical knowledge which can only be picked up on the job. This gender disparity has often resulted in women earning less than men.

Another problem now considerably eased by the recent economic boom and consequent labor shortage, was the difficulty unemployed women faced in finding full-time jobs once they exceeded the age of 40. So after the last child, many middle-aged women have not even looked for full-time work. This has left volunteer work, part-time jobs, or courses at local universities as their usual alternatives.

## MORE WORKING WOMEN

Today, however, Dutch culture is changing and there is a rapid increase in the total number of working mothers, most of them working part-time. In 1981, only 30% of women were working outside the house. By 1994 this figure had grown to 42% and in 1999, it was 58%. If the economy continues to do well, the number of working mothers is expected to rise to 64-67% over the next decade.

The reasons for this impressive change? To some extent there is now more economic necessity for both husband and wife to work if they want to live well, take interesting vacations and buy expensive worldly goods.

But probably more important is the fact that many women are now wanting a career of their own (other than housework) and the Dutch government has policies which encourage this trend. In the years ahead, having tasted the fruit of the financial independence which comes from having an income of their own, it seems unlikely Dutch women will want to turn back the clock. Dutch mothers may even find that a career and children are not necessarily incompatible if adequate child care facilities are made available.

## CHILDHOOD

### Raising Children

Before World War II, big families (10 or more children) were not uncommon in the predominately-Catholic southern part of the Netherlands. Since birth control was not widespread then, workers and rural folk of modest means often found themselves with very large families.

*A Dutch mother and son: children are encouraged to express themselves.*

But times change and having two to three children is now the norm. Birth control is practised universally. Some couples do not to marry because they think marriage is unnecessary, old-fashioned or too restrictive but they decide to have children nevertheless.

## *No Brat Pack*

Dutch children are raised very permissively rather than strictly. There are no gender differences here: boys and girls are brought up the same way because their parents think all human beings should be treated equally.

Parents expect that their children will be heard as well as seen and will have their say in family decisions. Most parents feel that children should have the freedom, within some loose limits, to say and do just what they please. This belief is echoed by TV programmes for children, which often poke fun at parents' relative conservatism and at society's many rules and regulations.

Strangely enough, such extreme permissiveness usually does not, in the long run, produce spoiled, bratty children. Most middle class parents (i.e., the vast majority of the population) do try, consciously or unconsciously, to conform to those "ideal" traits of Dutch character which we discussed in the chapter on how the Dutch see themselves. In so doing they set an example which the children themselves are quick to perceive as constituting "good" behaviour for which they will be praised.

## *Behaviour, Good and Bad*

What constitutes "good" behaviour for a Dutch child? Some examples: children are warmly praised for being polite, honest, straightforward, doing well at sports and getting passing if not top grades at school. They are mildly reproved for "bad" behaviour: not being able to amuse themselves, interrupting adult conversations to get attention, doing poorly at school, bullying other children or stealing.

The net result is that most of these free-spirited children will end up following the lead of their parents and will gradually evolve into hard-working, responsible, tolerant and well-mannered young adults – not barbarians or dropouts.

## *Teenagers*

It is worth mentioning, too, that while the Dutch do have a few problems with their teenagers, there is really not much of a generation gap in the Netherlands. As a result, teenage problems do not seem to be as overwhelming (for young people and parents alike) as they are in some other countries.

Indeed, Dutch teenagers seem to be a fairly conservative lot. Opinion surveys indicate that while only 25% of the 18-year olds think that a steady relationship is necessary before people sleep with each other, fully 50% of them are still virgins at that age.

## *Freedom to Choose*

Dutch parents are very tolerant. They do not expect that their children will necessarily follow in parental footsteps and do not put any real pressure on them to do so. Parents may try to steer children in one general direction or another, but young people are expected to orient themselves and are free to choose whatever professions or lifestyles they like. Well-educated parents, however, do hope that their children will look for jobs which involve a relatively high intellectual level of work.

## *Adoption*

Because of widespread birth control, few unwanted children are born in the Netherlands, so very few are available for adoption. If a suitable child can be found, the adoption process itself will take a long time (two to seven years) because of the careful background checks designed to prevent child abuse. There is no social or legal discrimination against adopted children.

## *Student Days*

The Dutch educational system is one of the best and most extensive in the world. It is strict, formally organized and gives students an exposure to different subjects. Knowing something about it can help you understand why the overall quality of life in the Netherlands is remarkably high.

It is so high simply because most Dutch men and women are quite competent professionally. This is not to say that they are more intelligent than other people in the world but that in most cases they know their jobs well and do them well. The underlying reason for this happy state of affairs is probably that they have been trained very well at school.

Indeed, compared to their counterparts in the US or UK, Dutch students do not have the luxury of simply drifting through school. They have to work very hard: most secondary school students must do two to three hours of homework every day. High standards mean that degrees are not obtained easily: the average graduate course lasts more than five years.

## *THE DUTCH EDUCATIONAL SYSTEM: AN OVERVIEW*

This educational system consists of primary schools; secondary schools, of which there are several kinds; vocational schools; special schools; institutes of higher learning; institutes of international education; and adult education schools.

By far the best introduction to the complicated details of the Dutch educational system is the Ministry of Education's excellent and well-organized booklet "Going to School in the Netherlands," which is published in eight foreign languages, including English, and is available from DOP, Postbus 11594, 2502 AN The Hague. This booklet is a must if you are planning to send your children to school in the Netherlands.

## *Primary Schools*

These are for children between the ages of 4 and 12. At first (during the first three years of primary school) the main emphasis is on the child's development. At the same time, a learn-by-playing curriculum introduces children to reading, writing and arithmetic. They also learn some elementary social and manual skills.

In the next five years they are taught Dutch, arithmetic, history, geography, environmental awareness and social science. All schools also teach art and have facilities for physical exercise. English is sometimes taught beginning in the last year of primary school. This is the reason so many Dutch speak (but not necessarily write) English so well: they began studying it at the age of 12.

## *Secondary Schools*

Children stay in secondary school from the age of 12 to 18. Several kinds of secondary schools are often housed in the same building so pupils can transfer from one type of education to another. All pupils, however, are taught the same 15 subjects in the first three years of secondary school. The various types of secondary school are:

- Schools for junior general secondary education (known by their Dutch initials as MAVO). These last four years and admit the student to senior vocational education.
- Schools for senior general secondary education (HAVO). These last for five years.
- Schools for pre-university education (VWO). These last for six years and prepare the student for university studies.
- Schools for pre-vocational secondary education (VBO). These last for four years and give the student a general education.

## *Vocational Education*

Pre-vocational training tailored individually for each student (IVBO) is also available.

## *Special Schools*

These teach mentally handicapped, physically disabled or malad-justed children or children with learning disabilities.

## *What Happens to School Dropouts?*

Not all Dutch students do brilliantly. They may be unruly and impatient or lack motivation. If in addition to these behaviour and attitude problems a student comes from a family with low educational levels, he or she has more likelihood of becoming a dropout.

In some developed countries, students who do poorly and drop out of secondary school are likely to end up unemployed (perhaps permanently) and may well turn to drugs or crime. Things are different in the Netherlands.

In the first place, students are simply not permitted to leave secondary school before the age of 16. If they do poorly at one school, they are transferred to a lower-level school and are given special attention. Work-study programs are also strongly encouraged.

Ultimately, however, it is the safety net provided by the Dutch welfare system that keeps teenage school-leavers from utter destitution and helps to reduce the appeal of drugs and crime.

In 1997, for example, an unmarried unemployed person under the age of 21 was eligible for f324 per month in "income support" plus an additional holiday allowance of f17 per month. A young person could not live on this total alone but if he or she also took advantage of all the other social benefits which are available, there would be no need to starve, sleep in the street or turn to drugs and crime.

So Dutch dropouts usually do not fail: in fact, 90% of them end up finding some kind of paid employment or go into some other field of education. The downside is that they often become flexi-workers and are faced with temporary jobs with reduced prospects of advancement.

## *Institutes of Higher Education*

The average level of education in the Netherlands has been rising sharply. Whereas only 15% of the men over 65 have a higher education, 27% of younger men between 25-44 have such qualifications. The increase in women's education has been even more striking. For those over 65, only 6% went beyond secondary school; for younger women aged 22-44, 22% have a higher education.

The race for educational qualifications continues because in the Netherlands today a good education is the keystone of career success. People therefore want more and more certificates of higher education.

This is posing a financial problem for the Dutch government, which is trying to contain this stream of people by cutting educational costs and by limiting the time students have to finish their studies. Schools feel the financial pinch, too, and are faced with having to make hard choices between the quality and quantity of education they offer.

There are 14 universities in the Netherlands (including the Open University, which offers correspondence courses) as well as numerous colleges for higher professional education. Leiden University, founded in 1575 by Prince William of Orange, is the oldest university in the Netherlands. Higher education studies begin at the age of 18.

The Dutch universities and colleges of higher education are financed by the state. In addition, there are seven theological colleges which are financed partly from government funds. Higher education, however, is not free.

The Dutch government gives students a stipend but this is not enough to cover all their expenses. In 1999, for example, the stipend was only about f500 per month, whereas the cost of university education was about f15,000 per year.

To make ends meet, university students must therefore ask for parental support, borrow money at low interest rates or get part-time jobs. Most of them prefer to find jobs rather than be a burden on their parents or go into debt. In 1996, however, a "results grant" was introduced. This means that students in higher education can begin by borrowing money. If their grades are good, these loans will become a grant or at least a partial grant.

University courses are given in two stages. The first lasts from four to six years and concludes with the *"doctoraal"* examination – hence the title "Drs" *(doctorandus)* which you will often see on Dutch business cards. The second stage, designed for the relatively few students who wish to become scholars or professors, involves highly specialized courses of study or research leading to a doctorate (Ph.D.).

## *Institutes of International Education*

Expatriates living and working in the Netherlands have a wide choice of schools for their children. Options for international education include: boarding schools, some coeducational; British, American, French and German schools; Dutch schools with a special English-language stream, e.g., for an International Baccalaureate; and regular Dutch schools.

An informative folder published by the Foundation for International Education (Stichting Internationaal Onderwijs, c/o Mr H L F 's-Gravesande, Prinses Irenelaan 11, 2341 TP Oegstgeest, Netherlands) gives many useful details. You should have a look at it if you plan to send your own children to an international school in the Netherlands.

## *Adult Education*

Adult education is becoming increasingly popular in the Netherlands and it is estimated that 37% of Dutch adults are enrolled in an educational course of some kind. Men tend to focus on practical, career-oriented subjects; women are more inclined to take courses on cultural subjects.

In addition to the Open University mentioned above, there are Adult Education Centres (Volksuniversiteit). You can also check with a local university to see if it offers part-time studies in English, for example, in the evening or during the day.

## *MARRIAGE*

### *Weddings*

Young men and women meet each other in their own social circles and at schools, clubs and bars. Statistically, educated people tend to marry somewhat later (at the age of 28-30) than less educated people, who marry at 20-22.

Most people will live together for a few years (with full parental blessing) before deciding to get married. Fifty-five per cent of women under the age of 27 have lived with a partner and usually decide to get married when they expect a baby.

When they do get married there are often two separate ceremonies.

The first is always a civil ceremony at the Town Hall. Legally, this is the only wedding that counts because it alone forges the bonds of marriage. But some people want a church wedding as well. However, a church ceremony is, so to speak, only frosting on the cake: the man and woman were already legally married at the Town Hall.

After the ceremony there is usually a reception for many guests, followed by a smaller gathering of the couple's family and closest friends.

Here the bride and groom (and perhaps their parents, too) must make very difficult social decisions as they plan these events. Dutch custom requires that the invitations sent to all the guests must state if they are invited to the smaller party. Those who are not invited may be unhappy. As one foreign resident of Amsterdam explains, "People who thought themselves close friends may be lost for life if they come down on the wrong side of the great divide."

### *Contracts*

A formal "contract of living together" is usually drawn up by heterosexual couples who live together but who do not want to get married. Legally, homosexuals are not permitted to marry (although in 1999 the Dutch Parliament approved a proposed law

THE CYCLE OF LIFE IN THE NETHERLANDS

permitting homosexual marriages). However, they, too, can draw up a formal contract which involves rights and obligations which are similar to marriage, except that adoption is not possible (although this may change in the future).

## *Divorce*

The Dutch are conservative about marriage, usually staying faithful to their partner and sometimes believing that a bad marriage is better than none at all.

Nevertheless, roughly 33% of all Dutch marriages will end in divorce, a figure which has been remained remarkably constant over the last 20 years. Divorces in the Netherlands are socially acceptable, relatively easy to get and, depending on the amount of money at stake and how long the squabbles go on, comparatively cheap. Children from the age of 12 on have a say in which parent they would like to live with. There are also a few "divorces of convenience" purely for tax reasons.

If they do have a troubled marriage, the Dutch do not turn instinctively to marriage counselling sessions or to other forms of therapy. These aids certainly exist but are not thought to do much good, at least in terms of saving the marriage itself.

## *MIDDLE AGE*

In the Netherlands today, as is the case in the US and UK, more and more middle age/middle management employees in their late forties and early fifties are being declared redundant or are being forced into early retirement.

This is because the traditional pyramidal structures of Dutch organizations are changing due to cost-cutting measures and to the information revolution ushered in by ever-faster computers. Nowadays there is no need for so many expensive older white collar employees. As a result, job uncertainty and job- hopping

82

have increased among them as the younger generation begins to take over.

The result is that today only 29% of 55- to 64-year-old workers are still on the job. Those who have left the full-time work force do not usually get a lucrative "golden handshake" – a Dutch banker joked to me that "they may get a handshake of some kind, but it won't be golden!"

Once out of the office, however, they will find that, thanks to the economic boom, getting a temporary job is relatively easy. Moreover, some people have saved to finance an early retirement. Thus, one way or another, retired people manage to make ends meet.

## RETIREMENT

The official retirement age is 65 but in practice it is actually 58 to 60; only 15% of 60 to 65 year old workers are still on the job. Both private employers and the Dutch government provide retirement benefits. People in the private sector claim that Dutch civil servants fare very well indeed and that their benefits are among the best in the world.

## OLD AGE, EUTHANASIA AND DEATH

Older parents do not live with their children. They first try to live on their own for as long as possible. Eventually they may move into a serviced flat, where one hot meal is provided each day. Later on, when they need more care they may move into a retirement home and, ultimately, into a nursing home. Government welfare payments and a small old age pension after 65 contribute to their financial support.

### Euthanasia

The Netherlands has a paradoxical policy on euthanasia. Legally, it is forbidden. In practice, however, if a doctor follows a number of carefully constructed guidelines and procedures, he or she will not be prosecuted for ending the life of a terminally ill patient.

83

## *Death*

When death occurs the Dutch do not arrange lavish funerals or engage in public displays of mourning, preferring instead to keep their feelings to themselves or within the family circle.

There will be a church service or a secular gathering at the *Uitvaartcentrum* ("departure centre"), either of which will be followed by a reception where coffee and cake are served. Subdued colours are worn – but not necessarily black, because this might be overdoing it. There are now slightly more cremations than burials.

*— Chapter Nine —*

# DUTCH CULTURE: THE GOLDEN AGE AND AFTERWARDS

The Netherlands has one of the richest cultures in the whole of Western Europe. Since a great deal has already been written about it in English and other languages (especially in the field of art history) we will be very selective here and will look at only three of its many aspects:

- The Dutch language itself: both spoken and body language.

- The arts: painting, music, architecture and design, literature, theatre, dance and the festivals celebrating them.

- The remarkable decline of "pillarization" (social compartmentalization), which had played such an important role in Dutch daily life.

## *THE DUTCH LANGUAGE*

More than 21 million Dutch and Flemish (Belgian) people speak Dutch, a Germanic language with many parallels with German and English. There are also Dutch speakers in northwest France and it is the language of education and government in the Netherlands Antilles, Aruba and Suriname. Because Indonesia was once a colony of the Netherlands, some senior Indonesian lawyers, officers and historians can speak it, too. And one of the languages of South Africa – Afrikaans – originates from the Dutch spoken in the 17th century.

Dutch, however, is not the only official language of the Netherlands: in the northern province of Friesland, Frisian is the mother tongue of some of the 620,000 Frisians. It is not a dialect of Dutch but a separate, though similar, language.

Unlike British English, in which even to the untutored ear of the foreigner one kind of accent is clearly upper class and another is clearly working class, the Dutch language reflects social differences more subtly.

Although the Netherlands today is overwhelmingly a middle class society and becoming more so all the time, there is nevertheless a well established and prosperous "old" upper middle class.

Much less visible is the Dutch aristocracy, which consists of 150-200 families with a total of 10,000 members. It is certainly in keeping with the Dutch tradition of social equality, however, that being an aristocrat doesn't mean very much, either to the public at large or to the aristocrats themselves. One titled Dutch lady I know even has her family crest tattooed on her wrist and rides a huge Harley-Davidson motorcycle!

These upper middle class and aristocratic Dutch men and women can be detected not so much by their worldly goods (they definitely do not believe in conspicuous consumption) but by the more refined Dutch they speak. Only a native speaker of Dutch, however, is likely to notice the slight differences in their speech.

For a foreigner, being able to read some Dutch is very useful indeed – for menus, shopping, newspaper headlines, road signs and travel by train, tram, bus or bicycle – but if you will be in the Netherlands for only a year or two, are not looking for a job and can make yourself understood in English, German or French, you won't actually need to speak much Dutch.

The more you know, the better, of course. For those with the time and aptitude, learning Dutch is certainly a good idea and will make your stay in the Netherlands easier and more enjoyable.

On the other hand, if you are looking for a job with a Dutch firm the ability to speak and read Dutch may well be a requirement. (Because English is so widely used in the Netherlands, proficiency in English is not a sought after skill and as such not very helpful in a job search.) Fortunately, there are many schools and individuals in the Netherlands which are well-qualified to teach Dutch.

But be warned: as soon as they perceive you are a foreigner the Dutch are very likely to address you in any language except Dutch. They take pride in showing off their knowledge of other languages and unless you can make really exceptional progress in mastering their own language – which is not a terribly easy one for most foreigners because of its guttural sounds and long words, e.g., *tewerkstellingsvergunning* (an employment permit) – the Dutch will probably want to communicate with you in English, German, French or whatever other language they suppose you speak best.

## *Body Language*

Unlike the Italians and some other nationalities, the Dutch do not use body language very much. In the formal portraits by Frans Hals and others, their ancestors are clearly stolid and impassive. The Dutch of today carry themselves in a more relaxed, informal way and are quicker with a smile than a frown, but they still value social restraint.

Perhaps for this reason the people of the Netherlands have never developed an extensive vocabulary of hand, facial or other gestures.

Only four exceptions come to mind. In moments of anger, tapping or pointing at the forehead with the index finger shows you think the person in question is mentally unbalanced. Tapping the side of the head with the index finger, however, is a way of saying that person is quite intelligent. As it is in other countries, a vertical middle finger, standing alone, is a highly insulting and obscene gesture. Finally, there is the *vermanende vingertje* (wagging index finger) mentioned earlier, which warns against laziness or mischief. In general, however, when the Dutch wish to communicate, they usually rely on words, not on body language.

## THE ARTS

### Painting

The Dutch take justifiable pride in what historians refer to as their "art mountain," much of which can be admired in the museums of Amsterdam, The Hague, Leiden, Utrecht, Haarlem and Rotterdam. Each artistic period, however, saw so many gifted painters at work that to reduce this embarrassment of riches to manageable size let us confine ourselves to only six artists. (If no museum is listed after a given painting, this means the work is no longer in the Netherlands.)

### A 16th Century "Primitive"

* ***Hieronymus Bosch*** (c. 1450-1516) has been described by art historians as "the most creative painter of fantasy who has lived." Bosch's best-known paintings include detailed and often grotesque pictures ("Hell," "Ship of Fools"), works of pure fantasy ("Adoration of the Magi") and paintings characterized by detached observation ("The Prodigal Son" found in the Boymans-van Beuningen Museum, Rotterdam).

## *Painters of the Golden Age (17th Century)*

- *Rembrandt van Rijn* (1606-1669) achieved great fame as a portraitist who could solve problems of light and shadow, as in "The Anatomy lesson of Dr Tulp" (in the Mauritshuis, The Hague). This shows a group of doctors, dressed chiefly in black, peering intently at the very pale cadaver being dissected before them. At the other end of the human spectrum, however, the warmth, love and tenderness of a good marriage are nearly palpable in "Jewish Bride" (in the Rijksmuseum, Amsterdam). The best known of Rembrandt's portraits, however, is certainly "The Night Watch" (also in the Rijksmuseum, Amsterdam), a huge painting showing the officers of the civic guard.

- *Frans Hals* (c. 1580-1666) vividly captured the stolid, no-non-sense, enduring qualities of Dutch gentlemen and ladies. Good examples of his work are "Portrait of Nicolaes Woutersz van der Meer" and "Cornelia Claesdr Vooght" (both in the Frans Halsmuseum, Haarlem) as well as the big-sky feeling of the Netherlands itself – "Duinlandschap met konijnenjacht" ("Dune landscape with rabbit-shooting") – which is also in the Frans Halsmuseum in Haarlem.

- *Johannes Vermeer* (1632-1675) was the master of muted light. What is arguably his finest work, "View of Delft" (in the Mauritshuis, The Hague), shows the city of Delft steeped in a soft golden light reflected from sky, clouds and water. On a more intimate scale, "Girl Reading" conveys a gentle luminous serenity.

## *19th and 20th Centuries*

- *Vincent van Gogh* (1853-1890), it is said, so despaired of foreign-ers being able to pronounce his last name correctly (it sounds something like *van Khokh*) that he signed his pictures with his first name alone. During one of his fits of insanity he cut off part of his

89

own ear. But van Gogh's bright pigments, inspired by the colours of southern France ("Cornfield and Cypress Trees"), and his tortured "Self Portrait" have earned him a lasting place in modern art.

* ***Piet Mondrian*** (1872-1944) was a founding member of the abstract art movement known as *De Stijl* (literally, The Style), which was centred in the Netherlands. The works of his mature period offer the viewer a carefully-calculated selection of cool, pure geometrical shapes. For example, Mondrian's 1929 "Composition with Red, Yellow, and Blue" (in the Gemeentemuseum, The Hague) is a square white canvas divided by bold black lines into a central white square flanked and balanced by three small red, yellow and blue rectangles.

## *Music*

Music has always been important to the Dutch. Indeed, the most famous organist and composer of the *Oude Kerk* (Old Church) in Amsterdam, J.P. Sweelinck (1562-1621), was a forerunner of J.S. Bach. Later Dutch achievements have been more along the lines of performing great music rather than actually creating it. Thus today the Royal Concertgebouw Orchestra in Amsterdam and the Residentie Orchestra in The Hague are two of the finest ensembles in the world. Opera flourishes in Amsterdam's Muziektheater.

Music is also widely available at less classical levels. Pop festivals are staged throughout the year in the Netherlands. The annual North Sea Jazz Festival in The Hague is always well-attended. And last but not least, Saturday shoppers in many Dutch cities can enjoy the rollicking tunes of the ornately decorated street organs, which are nearly identical to their 19th century predecessors and which are played on the street by itinerant musicians who will welcome a bit of your loose change.

## *Architecture and Design*

The solidly constructed and beautifully maintained 17th and 18th century houses lining the canals of major cities are architectural masterpieces still in daily use as offices and elegant private homes. In the 20th century, Dutch architects have turned their attention to urban development (chiefly in Amsterdam and Rotterdam), new towns (Almere and Zeewolde), rapidly growing areas (Zoetermeer) and official buildings (the long, low, modernist headquarters of the Dutch Institute for Architecture and Town Planning in Rotterdam).

The best known force in Dutch design was the Spartan, rigorously geometric *De Stijl* movement, a group of designers and artists who flourished in the 1920s. A classic example of their work is Gerrit Rietveld's famous armchair, which is now in Utrecht's Centraal Museum.

## *Literature*

Dutch contributions to world literature seem to have been greater in the past than in more recent times. In the Middle Ages, for example, Dutch writers produced (in Latin) Arthurian romances and animal allegories which were part of the fabric of Western European tradition. Erasmus' great 16th century work, *In Praise of Folly*, was widely translated. The Golden Age of the 17th century saw many Dutch writers at work and the 1637 publication of the authorised Dutch version of the Bible helped to solidify the Dutch language itself.

Subsequently, however, most Dutch writers, no matter how talented and well-known in their own country, could not attract a wider circle of non-Dutch readers because of the language barrier. Two major 19th century novelists, for example, were not easily accessible to foreign readers for a long time.

The first of these is Eduard Douwes Dekker (best known under his pseudonym, Multatuli, and for his book *Max Havelaar*), who heaped scorn upon Dutch colonial rule in what is now Indonesia. The other novelist is Louis Couperus, who dissected the bourgeois society of The Hague and who in *The Hidden Force* also wrote about the futility of the Dutch colonial enterprise.

A few modern Dutch writers, such as the historian Johan Huizinga *(The Waning of the Middle Ages)*, have been widely translated but most of the post-World War II generation of Dutch novelists have not. As a result, few if any well-read British or American readers are familiar with them.

But thanks to the efforts of the Association for the Production and Translation of Dutch Literature, more Dutch literary works are being translated into other languages. Now that this process is picking up speed, modern Dutch writers may at last become better known abroad. Examples of these authors are: Hermans, Mulisch, van het Reve, Haasse, Wolkers, Nooteboom, 't Hart and van der Heijden.

## *Theatre*

Since professional theatre companies in the Netherlands get part of their funding from the government, they can afford to offer a varied repertoire. There are many smaller companies too, some of which also get government support. They try to create new forms of theatre by bringing together music, mime and new media techniques. But since most theatre companies perform in Dutch, however, their appeal to foreigners is limited.

## *Dance*

There are major dance companies in, respectively, Amsterdam (the National Ballet), The Hague (the Netherlands Dance Theatre) and Rotterdam (the Scapino Ballet). The National Ballet specializes in classical ballets, while the other two companies perform more contemporary works. The many smaller dance companies, for their part, offer productions of modern dance.

## *Artistic Festivals*

The Holland Festival, held throughout the month of June, is the most prominent annual festival and has a broad international programme. Medieval and Baroque music are the highlights of the Holland Music Festival, held in Utrecht. The annual North Sea Jazz Festival in The Hague is known to jazz fans around the world. The Theatre Festival, held jointly in The Hague and Antwerp (Belgium), offers Dutch and Flemish stage productions.

Every other year, the Holland Dance Festival is held in The Hague. And to complement the Netherlands' own film industry (which has made some excellent documentaries), the Rotterdam Film Festival is held each year. A "Poetry International" festival is held annually in Rotterdam.

## *THE DECLINE OF PILLARIZATION*

For hundreds of years the Dutch had a unique way of organizing their own society. Known as "pillarization" *(verzuiling*, i.e., social compartmentalization), this was the practice of using religious or political affiliation as one of the basic "pillars" of Dutch life. Much of Dutch life was organized around this pillarization.

There were deep historical roots for this policy. After the Reformation and the establishment of Protestant churches in the 16th century, the northern part of the Netherlands inclined toward Protestantism (the Dutch Reformed Church was the major Protestant denomination) while the southern part of the country tended to remain Roman Catholic.

Designed to prevent religious discord, pillarization strongly encouraged Catholics, Protestants, liberals and socialists to follow parallel but separate paths through life.

In practice, this meant that there were Catholic schools, universities, trade unions, sports and social clubs; Protestant schools, universities, trade unions, sports and social clubs; and separate media outlets (television, radio and press) for the followers of each of these major beliefs.

The Dutch government, for its part, took pains to make sure that both Catholics and Protestants were always represented on official bodies. A Protestant solicitor from the north of the Netherlands, for example, might be appointed as the Public Prosecutor in Maastricht, a predominantly Catholic city in the south. In private life, however, some religious prejudice persisted: a Protestant homeowner might refuse even to consider selling his or her house to a Catholic.

But beginning in the 1960s, general prosperity and wider educational opportunities in the Netherlands gradually weakened the hold of organized religion on Dutch life. The growth of a secular society, a stronger national government and the waning of church influence all combined to cut the main props out from under the traditional policy of pillarization.

For centuries pillarization was the keystone in the arch of Dutch cultural life. Since the 1960s, however, there has been a slow, peaceful but nevertheless quite remarkable social change: pillarization has gone into a terminal decline. One proof of this great cultural shift is that young Dutch men and women now in their 20s will categorically deny that pillarization still exists at all.

## A Mixed Blessing?

Such an enormous sea-change in Dutch culture has had both good and bad effects. On the positive side of the ledger, the Dutch now have more personal freedom because they no longer need to rely exclusively on religiously or politically based organizations for their professional and social success.

At the same time, however, some Dutch commentators speculate that this loosening of social control may have contributed, if only indirectly, to an increase in personal anxiety, to greater vandalism and to more drug use by young people. Conceivably, they say, in the future it may also lead to more social isolation for older people, who will not have communal organizations to rely on for support.

*— Chapter Ten —*

# DUTCH CUSTOMS

You will understand the Dutch more easily if you know a little bit about some of their customs and habits. These would certainly include preserving the past; a reliance on rules and regulations; cleanliness; traditional food and drink; smoking; sorting rubbish; the importance of birthdays and *Sinterklaas* (Santa Claus).

## *ARTIFACTS OF A TREASURED PAST*

The Dutch of today do not worship the past but they certainly respect it and want to keep many parts of it alive.

They may not have any strong feelings about clogs (the traditional wooden shoes), although these are in fact quite useful for gardening because they do keep your feet warm and dry. Nor do they wax ecstatic about the colourful traditional Dutch costumes, such as those still worn by men, women and children in a handful of Dutch villages.

Such artifacts may provide great photo opportunities for the tourists who come to the Netherlands from all over the world but the Dutch themselves do not think of them as being vitally important aspects of national culture. What the Dutch do think worth cherishing and preserving at all costs are:

- The important natural features of their country, such as the De Hoge Veluwe National Park and the Wadden Islands, which can best be preserved by sensitive environmental management techniques.

- The extensive architectural heritage of the Netherlands. Into this latter category the Dutch would put all their fine old houses, historic streets, cafes, ships, dikes, canals, windmills, churches and traditional farmhouses.

## RULES AND REGULATIONS

A labyrinth of complicated rules and regulations protects almost all of this architectural heritage. Official planning permission is needed to make any significant changes to it and approval is not given lightly or quickly. Indeed, property owners can sometimes find themselves caught between conflicting official demands.

Take the *bruine cafés* ("brown cafes"), for example. These are old Dutch drinking spots darkened by decades or even centuries of tobacco smoke. One of the most famous in Amsterdam is the *Hoppe* in a city square known as *het Spui* ("the sluice"). This cafe opened its doors for business in 1670 and the Dutch have been drinking and smoking there ever since.

But there are a good number of less ancient brown cafes, too. The owner of one of them told me about the problems he was having with the front door of his cafe.

This brown cafe stands on a corner where two Amsterdam streets meet – let us call them Streets A and B. For many years the front door has opened onto Street A. Recently, however, the owner was told that to comply with fire regulations his front door had to be moved so that it opened onto Street B. Planning permission officials, however, insisted that the front door had to remain facing Street A – but that to restore the cafe's historic authenticity, the door would have to be relocated so that it was closer to the corner!

## CLEANLINESS AND GODLINESS

If Dutch homes are not the *very* cleanest in the world, they certainly must be very close to the cleanest. It may be stretching the point a bit to say that the Dutch have always tacitly considered cleanliness to be more important than godliness, but traditionally these two qualities have gone hand-in-hand.

A clean house, for example – so clean that the window curtains were always left open to show off the interior – was indisputable proof that a respectable Calvinist family lived within. Stripped of its religious overtones, this social pressure continues today. Curtains are still left open and most middle class housewives believe that maintenance standards in the home must be kept very high; if they are not, the neighbours would surely talk.

## TRADITIONAL FOOD AND DRINK

If it can be said of the French that they "live to eat," then the Dutch "eat to live." Their day does not revolve around food and drink. Just as long as there is enough of everything, the Dutch are likely to be satisfied.

As you can imagine, this very practical, down-to-earth approach to eating has not created one of the world's great cuisines. Instead, Dutch food tends to be unsophisticated, hearty, filling and bland. If you yearn for exotic or spicy flavours, you must do as the Dutch themselves do and go out to an Indonesian or some other kind of ethnic restaurant – of which there are fortunately a great many in the Netherlands.

Even if Dutch cooking is never going to shoulder aside French, Italian, Spanish, Chinese or Indian cuisine, it does have its own simple charms. And since you will certainly be introduced to it during your stay in the Netherlands, this is a good time to make our way through the Dutch culinary day.

## *Breakfast*

The Dutch like a cold (uncooked) breakfast. On the well-laden table you may find several kinds of sliced bread (sandwich loaf, rye bread, raisin bread, etc., known collectively as *boterhammen)*; butter or margarine, jam and perhaps peanut butter or chocolate flakes (these flakes are a uniquely Dutch topping for bread); two or three kinds of sliced meats (ham, beef or salami); a selection of cheeses, which are to be thinly sliced with a cheese knife; and probably some dry breakfast cereals as well. Everything (except the cereals, of course) is eaten with knife and fork – not made into a sandwich and eaten with the hands.

To drink, there will always be tea or strong filter coffee (never instant coffee) invariably served with *koffiemelk*, a thick evaporated milk; orange juice or another fruit juice; and lots of milk or buttermilk *(karnemelk)* for the children.

A word here about cheese since it is one of things the Dutch do best. Cheese is never served at the end of a meal but is instead the real mainstay of breakfast and lunch. Some Dutch people eat a kilo (2.2 lbs) of cheese a week.

There are many different types of cheese on display in Dutch cheese shops and it is well worthwhile to ask the shop attendants about them. Some are semi-creamy when *jonge kaas* (young cheese) and drier when they are *belegen* or *oude kaas* (mature or old cheese). Edam cheese, shaped into a ball, is as popular in the Netherlands as it is abroad but often is not covered by the well-known red skin. Gouda cheese is wheel-shaped and flat. Other cheeses include *Leidse kaas* (Leiden cheese, flavoured with caraway seeds) and *Friese nagelkaas* (Friesland cheese, flavoured with cloves).

*A Dutch cheese shop in the city of Zeist. Dutch cheeses are known the world over.*

## Lunch

The Dutch allow themselves only 45 minutes for their lunch, which is usually eaten around 12:30 p.m. Often called a *koffietafel* (coffee table), it starts with a hot or cold snack, followed by a variety of breads and toppings. It may also consist of *broodjes* (soft rolls filled with meat or cheese and eaten like a sandwich) or an *uitsmijter* (two fried eggs and slices of cheese or ham or roast beef on top of two pieces of bread).

## Dinner

Dinner is the main meal of the day and is usually served relatively early – between 6:00 - 7:00 p.m. After their light meal at lunch, the Dutch are ready to tuck into some hearty fare in the evening. Because they travel so much and are so internationally minded, they can cook a wide range of European foods, but here are some of the very traditional Dutch dishes you may encounter.

- *Erwtensoep:* A warming winter green pea soup with sausage, which should be so thick, as the saying goes, that a spoon can stand upright in it.
- *Bruine bonen met spek:* Brown beans with bacon.
- *Boerenkool met rookworst:* Mashed potatoes, kale and smoked sausage.
- *Haring* (herring): The first herrings of the year *(nieuwe haring)* which are gutted and kept in brine, appear in the spring and are served with chopped onions. When bought from fish stalls on the street, they are traditionally eaten by holding the fish above one's mouth by the tail and eating it uncooked. The first cask of herrings is ritually offered each year to the queen.
- *Gerookte paling* (smoked eel): This is delicious as a starter or a quick snack on the street, where at fish stalls it is put into a soft roll *(broodje)*. In Friesland and North Holland you may even be invited to a smoked eel party, where the eels are smoked, peeled and then eaten whole.
- *Bitterballen:* Small meat croquettes, served as an appetizer.
- *Pannenkoeken* (pancakes): Sometimes huge, they can be topped by many different kinds of fillings.
- *Vis* (fish): Excellent fresh seafood is available in the Netherlands. *Tong* (sole), *schol* (plaice), *tarbot* (turbot), *zeewolf* ("sea wolf"), and Zeeland oysters and mussels are good choices.
- *Hutspot:* Beef stew with potatoes, carrots and onions. This dish dates from 1573, when it was prepared for the starving citizens of Leyden during the siege of that city.
- *Appelgebak:* Dutch apple pie, a superb snack or dessert usually served with *slagroom* (whipped cream).
- *Oliebollen* (oil balls): Round doughnuts with raisins, dusted with fine sugar, which are a New Year specialty.

## *Drinks*

The Dutch are notoriously fond of strong filter coffee *(koffie)* served with milk and sugar. They also enjoy sherry as an aperitif and sometimes drink wine with their dinner. Wine, however, is not cheap in the Netherlands and therefore is not, as it is in France, an invariable accompaniment to a meal.

Dutch beer – of which there is a wide range, differing not only in taste but also in strength – is really excellent. Some traditional alcoholic drinks, however, may be more of an acquired taste. These include *advocaat*, a very thick eggnog occasionally enjoyed by ladies after a heavy day of shopping, and several kinds of *jenever* (Dutch gin), which is usually served ice-cold in a small shot glass *(borrel)* filled literally to the brim.

## *Restaurants*

There are more than 900 restaurants in Amsterdam alone; other Dutch cities – notably The Hague and Rotterdam – are not far behind. Going out to dinner, whether at a local cafe or, more rarely, at an expensive restaurant, is a favourite Dutch pastime. You may be invited by Dutch friends. If so, remember that unless the host indicates otherwise, dining out is usually "Dutch treat," meaning that you will have to pay for your share of the bill.

When you tire of the blandness of traditional Dutch food, go find a good *chinees-indisch* ("Chinese-Indonesian") restaurant and order an Indonesian *rijsttafel* ("rice table"). This is a fabulous meal of rice accompanied by many different side-dishes from which you pile spicy helpings of exotic meats, fish, fruits and vegetables and mix everything together. Dutch beer is, of course, mandatory.

In the past, when colonial officials in the Dutch East Indies sat down to a proper *rijsttafel*, a long line of barefoot "boys" (waiters) each carried in one of these side-dishes – for example, small plates of chicken curry, green pepper, dried fish, coconut, onion, pepper, pineapple, nuts, raisins, bananas and hard-boiled eggs. Once, when

101

the Dutch Governor gave a formal banquet for the Sultan of Djokjakarta (Indonesia), there were 55 "boys" in line!

## *A TOBACCO CULTURE*

The paintings of the Golden Age show us that a Dutchman of that era, taking his ease in a tavern or at home, was rarely without his long-stemmed clay pipe. In more recent times the Dutch have continued to be avid smokers. If you are a nonsmoker, you may find it ironic that despite the fact the Dutch are very health-conscious on the whole, their houses, flats, restaurants and bars are rarely smoke-free.

Dutch smokers usually prefer cigarettes, often rolling them by hand from shag tobacco (a coarse tobacco cut into fine shreds) because this is the cheapest way to smoke. Some men are fond of the small Dutch cigars or, more rarely, a briar pipe.

Smoking in the Netherlands is inversely related to education: the more educated a Dutch person, the less likely it is that he or she smokes. So while fully 54% of the people with only secondary educations are smokers, only 33% of more highly educated people now smoke. After the age of 45, cigarette smokers become more inclined to quit. At the same time, however, there has been what an official Dutch report calls "an alarming rise" in the number of young smokers between 15 and 19 years old.

## *PROTECT THE ENVIRONMENT: SORT YOUR RUBBISH!*

Environmental protection is a vitally important issue in the Netherlands because the country is so small and so densely populated. As a result, the Dutch have become a very disciplined people when it comes to sorting their rubbish.

They are required by law (and you will be, too) to separate rubbish into specific categories – organic materials, inorganic substances, glass, paper, and chemical wastes (paint, batteries, etc.) – and put it into separate bins. Deposit glass (used in soft drink and beer bottles and for which you are charged money) is returned to specified sites for cash or credit. About 75% of the non-deposit glass is recycled for other uses.

## NEVER FORGET A BIRTHDAY

For the Dutch (young and old alike) birthdays are major cultural events. Forgetting a birthday is such a major blunder that in most Dutch homes you will find a "birthday calendar" hanging on the door of the toilet, where it can be pondered frequently and at leisure.

To celebrate his or her birthday, a child may get presents in the morning. He or she will bring candy to school to give to other children. Later in the day, parents always give a party for the child. The whole family comes and joins in happy birthday songs and ritualized congratulations to the fortunate child.

In a marked departure from the custom in some other countries, an adult celebrates his or her own birthday by inviting other people over for drinks or by giving a birthday party. And if you are working in an office, you are even expected to bring birthday cakes to the office so that your colleagues can participate in this festive occasion, too.

## SINTERKLAAS AND CHRISTMAS

In December the Dutch celebrate not only Christmas (25 December) but also St. Nicholas Day (December 5) as well. This is the day when good children get presents.

All Dutch children and adults know that every year *Sinterklaas* (St Nicholas) comes to the Netherlands from Spain by ship, arriving in Amsterdam. He is always riding a white horse and is dressed as a bishop because he is supposed to be the Bishop of Myra (Turkey), the patron saint of children, young women and sailors.

One or two naughty servants known as *Zwarte Piet* (Black Peter) always come with St Nicholas and carry canes with which to punish children who have done wrong. The discovery of *pepernoten* (round biscuits made of gingerbread) in the house is clear proof that *Zwarte Piet* has been there.

Several days before St Nicholas Day, Dutch children put a shoe by the fireplace so that *Sinterklaas* can leave a small present in it. On the evening of 5 December, presents are given to adults and children alike, often accompanied by short humorous poems on family themes.

This is also the time to eat such traditional delicacies as *borstplaat* and *speculaas* (different kinds of sweets), *taai-taai* (biscuits and cakes in various shapes and sizes) and *boterletters* or *chocoladeletters* (letters of the alphabet created from almond paste or chocolate).

Dutch settlers brought many of these customs to Nieuw Amsterdam (now New York) in the 17th century. Over the years their own *Sinterklaas* gradually evolved into the Santa Claus who is so familiar today.

# Chapter Eleven

# LIVING IN THE NETHERLANDS

This chapter is a potpourri of practical information which will hopefully be useful to you from the moment you first decide to move to the Netherlands. It covers a wide range of items:

- Getting a good start
- How should foreigners behave?
- Housing
- Travel: by air, land and water
- Documents needed
- Money
- Medical care
- Telecommunications and electrical equipment
- Leisure activities
- Religion
- Pets
- Emergencies

## *GETTING A GOOD START*

The ideal way to find your footing quickly in the Netherlands is to have Dutch friends who are willing to help and advise you. But it can take some time to make friends and it is never too early to start looking for them.

One very good reason to start early is that if you are like most people, your second or third month in any foreign country may well prove to be the most difficult. By then the initial starry-eyed excitement of travel to and arrival in the Netherlands will have worn off but you will not yet have had time to find your own particular niche in Dutch society. So making a concerted effort in the first month to make some Dutch friends may pay big dividends later on.

Fortunately, it is quite easy to meet people in the Netherlands. The Dutch like to live very busy lives but neighbours, office colleagues or local officials can always find time to answer your questions or point you in the right direction. Virtually all of them will speak at least some English and, being world travellers, most of them are also quite interested in foreigners. Indeed, it is likely that many of the people you meet will have already visited your own country.

One can recommend a three-step approach to integrating yourself into Dutch society: (1) meet your neighbours, (2) get in touch with some of the many social organizations designed to help newcomers to the Netherlands and (3) join a Dutch sports club. This three-pronged approach cannot, of course, guarantee that you will make some good Dutch friends but the chances of this happening are rather high. What is certain is that if you merely sit around waiting for the Dutch to come to you, your tour of duty in the Netherlands may be over before they do.

### *Step One: Meet Your Neighbours*

A French lady once moved to another West European country (not the Netherlands). After several years there she still had not met her next-door neighbour. So one fine morning she decided to knock on the neighbour's door and introduce herself. Being fluent in the local language she was able to do this with the utmost politeness, "Good morning, madame," she said, "I am your next-door neighbour." Imagine her surprise when her neighbour said to her brusquely, "Well, what is it that you want?"

Such a reply would be unheard of in the Netherlands. Indeed, it is up to you to make the first move. Your Dutch neighbours will not force themselves upon you but they will naturally be curious about you and will be very pleased if you will take the first opportunity to introduce yourself and tell them where you are from and why you are in their country.

It is certainly appropriate for you to invite them to your own house for coffee (at almost any time of the day, but around 10:30 a.m. is best) or for a drink in the evening. But to avoid any cross-cultural misunderstandings you should not use a "California-style" invitation – that is, a vague invitation cast in such general terms ("Do come see us!") that it is really only an expression of good will rather than a firm social commitment. Instead, try to find a mutually convenient date and time while you are first talking with your new neighbour.

## Step Two: Get in Touch with a Social Organization for Foreigners

Your own embassy, consulate or company may well have some good suggestions on living in the Netherlands but the international women's clubs are likely to be even better sources of information. They also offer a wide variety of social activities where you can easily "meet-and-greet" other people, foreigners and Dutch alike.

Fortunately, there is no shortage of these clubs. To list just a few of them: the American Women's Club, the British Women's Club, the Petroleum Wives Club, the Australian and New Zealand Women's Club and the international women's association known as Contact.

One social organization in The Hague which has been highly recommended is ACCESS (the Administrative Committee to Coordinate English-Speaking Services). Located at Societeit de Witte, Plein 24, 2511 CS The Hague, ACCESS is a non-profit organization staffed by English-speaking multinational volunteers. In addition to social functions, among the many support activities it offers are advice on settling in, counselling services and information on language development for bilingual children.

## *Step Three: Join a Dutch Sports Club*
Even if you are not keen on participating in sports yourself, one of the very best ways to meet the Dutch is to join one of their sports clubs. Some other countries may have an extensive network of sports facilities which are open to the public but this is usually not the case in the Netherlands. As a general rule, to participate in a sport there you must be a member or a guest of a local sports club. This is why in such a small country there are no less than 35,000 sports clubs with a total membership of 4.3 million people.

In descending order of their size, the major clubs are those devoted to fishing, football (i.e., soccer, the Dutch national sport), tennis and field hockey. But there are also clubs for almost all other activities – for example, water sports (sail and power boating, canoeing, surfing, swimming, boat trips and water skiing), cycling, horseback riding, hiking, steam trains, ice skating, bird watching, caravan trips, golf, and automobile and motorcycle racing. For the more sedentary, card clubs are very popular, too.

## *HOW SHOULD FOREIGNERS BEHAVE IN THE NETHERLANDS?*

You should keep in mind that Dutch society revolves around three simple themes:

- **Tolerance** – Letting people do things their own way as long as they do not disturb others.

- **Honesty and straightforwardness** – When you say "yes" or "no" you must mean precisely that, not "maybe," "perhaps" or "we shall see later on." This is important because in many other cultures it is considered extremely impolite to give a blunt "yes" or "no" answer. If you happen to come from one of these cultures you must now begin to practice the painfully direct Dutch approach.

- **Hospitality** – Making a guest feel comfortable and at home.

### *Major Social Sins*

You can immediately understand from this short list that a foreigner who wants to get along well with the Dutch must make every effort not to come across as prejudiced, devious or antisocial. These are major sins which are not easily forgiven.

### *Lesser Social Sins*

Although the Dutch usually like foreigners on a one-to-one basis, they do not appreciate group tourism because it is noisy and brings out what they consider to be some of the foreigners' less desirable traits. These the Dutch would list as flashiness, overconfidence, self-assertiveness, boisterous behaviour and bragging about wealth. You would do very well to avoid these failings, too.

In this connection and taking a page out of classical history, a Dutch journalist in Amsterdam once joked that some of his colleagues consider the Americans, in all their pride and economic, cultural and military might, to be "the new Romans" of our era. In contrast, he continued, the Dutch like to think of themselves as "the old Greeks" – that is, as a much better-educated and more highly cultured people who are no longer at the centre of world affairs.

## Greeting Each Other

People shake hands very frequently in the Netherlands and a short, warm firm handshake is more valued than a long, tepid limp-wristed grip. When you come into a room, shake hands with all the adults you know. You will probably quickly be introduced to the others but if not, you can introduce yourself by name and with a handshake.

Good friends usually greet each other by kissing each other, very lightly, on the cheeks two or three times, first on one side and then on the other. (This is actually not so much a real kiss as it is a quick touching of cheeks.) In any case, there is one important exception to this: although men may kiss women and women may kiss each other, heterosexual men never kiss other men.

## INVITATIONS AND GOOD MANNERS

### Morning Coffee

If invited to a friend's house for coffee around 10:30 a.m., you will be offered one *kopje koffie* (cup of coffee) with milk and sugar and one biscuit. When these are finished you will usually be offered a second cup of coffee, again with one biscuit. After this very Dutch ritual, it is time to take your leave.

### Lunch

Invitations for lunch are not as common in the Netherlands as in some other countries. Working people have only a short lunch break and must content themselves with a sandwich or a quick snack; women at home must prepare lunch for their own children. If you do not get invited to lunch, these will probably be the reasons.

## Pre-dinner Drinks

"Come for drinks" *(op de borrel)*, is a familiar invitation. This means you should arrive at your friend's house at about 5:30 p.m. A choice of wine, beer, jenever or sherry may be offered, as well as snacks. Since you have not been invited for dinner, you should leave by about 7:00 p.m.

## Dinner and Afterwards

The Dutch value their privacy at home and do not extend dinner invitations lightly. Being invited to a Dutch home for dinner is therefore a sign that the host and hostess think well of you and would like to see more of you. For this reason if for no other you should be on your best behaviour.

The Dutch eat dinner, the main meal of their day, relatively early. An invitation for 6:30 p.m. means you are being invited for dinner. You will first be offered a selection of alcoholic and nonalcoholic drinks (the host will tell you what is on offer) together with cheese crackers or snacks and will then be given dinner.

An invitation for 8:00 p.m., on the other hand, means only coffee and biscuits, usually followed by drinks and a very light snack. If there is any doubt in your mind about what the hostess has planned, you should telephone her to confirm this is an invitation for coffee.

In any case, whenever you do come it is absolutely essential that you be on time (the Dutch are very punctual) and that you bring a small but good quality present for the hostess – a bunch of flowers or a potted plant (widely available from local florists) are the most common gifts but a little box of chocolates, some decorative candles or a bottle of wine are equally acceptable. But don't overdo it: the Dutch value moderation in all things and bringing an extremely expensive bottle of rare wine would be a bit too much.

The Dutch like to dress informally. Few men wear suits nowadays; grey flannel trousers with a sport coat are much more common and can be worn to dinner. For a more formal dinner at the home of his boss, however, a man might decide to wear a tie as well. To be on the safe side, call beforehand to check.

Children may be present at a family dinner. Even if tempted to do so, do not try to discipline them if they are being noisy or are commenting to each other or to their parents in Dutch about your foreign appearance or strange table manners – this task should be left to the parents.

It is only good manners, of course, to resist any temptation to ask the host or hostess personal questions or to brag about how much you earn or what worldly goods you have. Nor should you criticize the royal family. The Dutch are not a flag-waving, highly nationalistic people but they are quietly patriotic nonetheless. Even accurate and well-meant "constructive" criticisms by foreigners may not be appreciated.

Until then it is best to confine yourself to complaining about the ever-increasing traffic congestion, the frequently terrible weather or the very high taxes.

And just as it is important that you arrive on time, it is important that you be ready to depart on time unless your host and hostess urge you to stay on. Be polite and do not overstay your welcome: be sure to leave when the coffee or liquor refills stop.

## HOUSING

The Netherlands is the most densely populated country in Europe. It already has a large number of single households and this number is increasing rapidly because more people are choosing not to marry, while others are deciding to divorce.

Housing is therefore much in demand. It is hard (but not impossible) to find and is always expensive. Rental prices will of course vary considerably but in good locations they are at least what you would have to pay in a comparable British or American city.

*Because stairways in old Dutch houses are very steep and narrow, beams projecting from the roofs were used to lift furniture and other heavy objects.*

Left to their own devices, most of the Dutch – especially those with young children – would much prefer to live in a small well-built semidetached house with a garden in one of the many charming towns on the fringes of the big cities. In practice, however, for financial or other reasons (commuting) many people decide instead to live in flats (apartments) located within or close to the city where they work. These flats can be found in both modern purpose-built structures and in big older homes which have been carved up into smaller units.

## Renting vs Buying

Because of the high transaction costs involved (taxes, etc.) it does not make financial sense to even think about buying a place of your own unless you plan to live in the Netherlands for at least four years.

The Dutch have never believed in the economic or social necessity of owning your own home. Traditionally, more than half the Dutch have lived in rented accommodation. One fundamental reason was that houses were expensive to buy and usually did not rapidly appreciate in value. Now, however, thanks to increasing rents and falling interest rates, the Dutch are becoming somewhat more inclined to buy houses rather than rent them.

## Location, Location, Location

As in any country, these are the three rules of finding a good place to live. It is up to you to do your homework (friends and colleagues can help you here) and get at least a rough idea just where you would like to live so you can identify the area by name – for example, "I would like to see some houses in Wassenaar." (This is a posh town close to The Hague which is favoured by senior executives.)

## Your Estate Agent

To rent or buy housing you will almost certainly need the services of a *makelaar* (estate agent). Your neighbours, friends or office colleagues are likely to know someone in this business, which is probably the best way to find a competent estate agent. But you can also come in off the street and talk with an estate agent whose office is located near where you would like to live.

Because your stay in the Netherlands might be curtailed by forces beyond your control – job transfers, illnesses, family problems, etc. – it is important to make sure there is a "diplomatic clause" in any rental agreement you sign. This will let you move out of the house on two months notice.

## Dutch Houses

So many things are small-scale in the Netherlands that you should not be surprised to find that except for the few merchant mansions or stately homes still in private hands, most Dutch houses are relatively small. If you are used to living in a big house filled with big furniture you may feel a bit cramped at first but this feeling will soon pass.

There may be one exception, however – the very steep staircases which are so common in older Dutch homes will not get any easier to negotiate. These traditional stairs, in fact, are the reason Dutch craftsmen made sure that the heavy ornately-carved wooden cabinets they built could be disassembled easily: once a cabinet was in pieces it could be hoisted from the street to a window on an upper floor by means of a pulley attached to a beam projecting from the top of the house.

Dutch houses are usually offered for rent unfurnished and to an American or British eye they may seem spartan in the extreme. For example, they may need wallpapering or interior repainting. They will not have any household appliances, floor coverings, curtains, lamps, etc.. There may not be any built-in lighting fixtures.

If you want a few more worldly goods in your new home, look for semi-furnished housing instead, which may well have light fixtures, some kitchen appliances and fitted carpets.

*Top: Elegant mansions were initially built as private residences but are now often used as offices or museums.*

*Bottom: Traditional Dutch houses are carefully maintained.*

You can of course move into a fully furnished home without having to provide too many things yourself besides bed linens and towels.

## DOMESTIC HELP

Because the Netherlands is such a prosperous and highly egalitarian society, almost no one has live-in servants. For most people, a nanny is prohibitively expensive because an employer must pay not only her salary but also her social security coverage. Because most mothers stay at home to care for their children, there is also a pronounced shortage of convenient child care facilities. You can, however, find part-time cleaning ladies through advertisements in the local newspapers.

## TRAVEL: BY AIR, LAND AND WATER

Perhaps because the Dutch are Europe's greatest travellers, they have taken pains to make sure that travel to, from and within the Netherlands itself is safe, fast, efficient, well-organized and affordable. Their public transportation is, in a word, excellent: it is certainly one of the best systems in the world.

### Travel by Air

The biggest Dutch airport is Schiphol, located southwest of Amsterdam and built on the bed of a former lake (the *Haarlemmermeer*) which was drained at the turn of the century and transformed into a *polder*, that is, into prime agricultural land.

Served by Dutch national carrier KLM and 79 other scheduled airlines flying to 220 destinations in more than 100 other countries, Schiphol now handles more than 36 million passengers each year. It is an outstandingly efficient, clean, user-friendly airport with good shops and good food. It offers easy access to Dutch and other European cities via a dense network of motorways and railways. There is even a railway station within the terminal itself.

Schiphol has become so popular, especially with transit passengers who account for nearly 40% of total passenger movements, that the Dutch have drawn up ambitious but environmentally-sensitive plans to expand it into a Mainport, i.e., a hub of intercontinental and European air, road and rail traffic.

Options under discussion include adding a fifth runway, creating an artificial island off the coast or even building a new airport. It is also hoped that once high speed trains (see below) are in wider use in the Netherlands, travellers bound for other European cities will decide to go by rail rather than by air, thus reducing the passenger burden on Schiphol itself.

International airlines offer regular services to some other airports in the Netherlands as well – to Rotterdam, Eindhoven and Maastricht.

## *Travel by Land*

### *Trains*

The Netherlands has a fabulous railway network. With 380 stations it is the most closely-knit in Europe and can boast of clean, fast, modern trains (many with snacks and refreshments on offer) linking all parts of the country. At least two trains an hour operate on each route; four to six trains per hour run between the major cities. Indeed, nearly every place in the Netherlands is accessible by train.

Since English is so widely spoken it is quite easy to travel by train. One of the best innovations is a useful service one can describe as "computerized directions." This is how it works:

Let us assume that you live in Amsterdam but have an appointment in Rotterdam at a given time. When you buy a ticket, if you tell the ticket agent when you have to be in Rotterdam, he or she will upon request give you not only a ticket but also a free computer printout showing the arrival and departure times of the most convenient trains for your journey, their track numbers and the details of any interstation transfers you may have to make.

*Second class railway carriage: clean, comfortable and fast.*

Armed with this handy printout you can turn your attention to other more interesting matters, rather than worrying about the logistics of rail travel.

Regular tickets can be bought at the *Binnenland* (domestic) ticket office at every Dutch station or from ticket machines. There are first and second class seats; a day return trip ticket is always cheaper than two single tickets.

Rail passes and special discounts are widely available. The *Euro Domino* pass, available from the *Internationaal* (international) ticket office at any one of 60 main stations, gives you three, five or ten days of unlimited rail travel in the Netherlands. Day tickets give you a day's unlimited travel, while *Rail Idee* (rail idea) tickets are available for visits to museums and other tourist attractions. Group tickets *(Meerman's kaart)* offer budget travel for a group of up to six people. Senior citizens and children get special fares, too.

Another excellent innovation is the *Treintaxi* (train-taxi), available at over 80 railway stations and serving more than 400 villages, town and cities – except for Amsterdam, Rotterdam and The Hague, where you can take local taxis. Here is how this service works:

Treintaxi tickets can be bought only at railway ticket offices, not in the taxi itself. When you buy your ticket you pay a small additional fixed charge. A taxi will be at your destination and will deliver you to any address in the surrounding area. Since you will be sharing the taxi with other travellers going to different addresses, the cost per person is quite low.

The Dutch are improving their railway network all the time. By about 2005, for example, a high speed rail connection called HSL *(Hoge Snelheids Lijn)* will link the Randstad with France and Germany. When this new system is in place, travellers may well decide to go by high speed train rather than by plane: from Amsterdam it will take only three hours to get to Paris, three hours to Frankfurt and two hours to Cologne. In 2005 also, a new double-track rail line for freight, the Betuweroute, will link the port of Rotterdam directly with the

European hinterland. This railway will strengthen the position of the Netherlands as a distribution and transport country. Freight by rail is forecast to rise from 20 million tons in 1990 to 65 million tons in 2010.

## *Automobiles*

If you live in the heart of Amsterdam or in one of the other big cities you can get by without owning a car because the public transportation network is so good. Not having a car will spare you the experience of Dutch traffic jams, which are bad now and are expected to get even worse as the number of cars on the road increases.

One creative measure to reduce traffic congestion is the introduction of Rekeningrijden (road pricing), which should be in operation by 2002. This involves using electronic fee collection systems to levy a fee on cars entering or leaving the major cities during rush hours. (Tourists may not be subject to these fees.)

Outside the big cities, however, a car is really quite useful. A wide range of makes and models is available but prices are high and repairs, insurance, road tax and petrol are all expensive. As a result, the smaller European or Japanese cars are more popular than big American vehicles. If you decide to rent a car, remember that almost all rental cars are equipped with manual rather than automatic transmissions.

If you want to bring your present car with you, first check to confirm that it can be brought in duty-free as part of your household goods. Make sure, too, it is a type already in use in the Netherlands. Otherwise you may find it expensive and very time-consuming (up to one year) to get it registered.

## *Driving License and Insurance*

If you are a national of an EU country you will only need your national driving license but within six months of arrival you must exchange it for a Dutch license. If you are not from the EU you may need an international driving licence, obtainable in most countries upon presentation of your national licence, but will have to exchange it for a Dutch license. An international license is obtainable within the Netherlands from the ANWB (see below). If you bring a car into the Netherlands or buy one there, you will need third party insurance (this is required by law) but more comprehensive insurance cover is strongly recommended. The minimum age for driving is 18 for cars and 16 for mopeds.

Once equipped with a car, license and insurance you are ready to sally forth onto Dutch roads. Fortunately, driving in the Netherlands poses no special risks or challenges for a newcomer who is used to driving in other developed countries.

Traffic moves on the right. Most Dutch drivers are competent and disciplined – perhaps more so in the country than in the frustratingly heavy traffic of the cities. One of their few bad habits is impatience: they do not make allowances for drivers who may not know precisely how to get where they are going. Tailgating (following behind a car too closely) can be another fault.

## Speed Limits

There are 2,360 km (1,466 miles) of toll-free motorways *(autosnelweg)*. Many of these roads are surprisingly quiet because a special macadam mixture is used to reduce tyre noise. The maximum speed limit is

either 120 kph (74 mph) or 100 kph (62 mph), depending on the area. Other speed limits are 50 kph (31 mph) in built-up areas and 80 kph (49 mph) on provincial roads.

Speed limits are enforced by police on fast BMW motorcycles, backed up by numerous speed traps and radar detectors. Fines are high if you are caught speeding and you can lose your license as well. During weekends and holidays there are many checks for alcohol, drugs, and weapons.

## *The ANWB*

You should consider becoming a member of a truly excellent organization for motorists (and for tourists, cyclists and caravaners as well)—the Royal Dutch Touring Association, known as the ANWB. Its affiliate, the Wegenwacht (WW) patrols the main roads and will assist you if your car breaks down. It will respond to telephone calls from the emergency roadside telephones. The ANWB also signposts itineraries through the most interesting towns and regions, provides maps and expert advice.

## *Caravans*

Caravans (house trailers) are exceptionally popular in the Netherlands because they provide convenient low-cost family accommodation on long trips. The Dutch are the greatest users of caravans in Europe and are possibly the most expert and the most friendly. It is easy for foreigners to join them: you can either rent a caravan in the Netherlands or bring your own. The documentation valid in the caravan's country of origin is all that is required.

Well-organized in this as in all their other leisure pursuits, Dutch caravaners will almost certainly be members of one of the many caravan clubs in their country. If they want to buy a second-hand caravan, the ANWB stands ready to give them technical advice on its particular strengths and weaknesses.

123

*Central railway station in Amsterdam.*

## *Bus, Tram and Metro*

For those coming to the Netherlands from countries where public transportation is either spotty or nonexistent, using the well-ordered Dutch "zone" network of buses and trams and the metro (the latter in Amsterdam or Rotterdam only) will be an eye-opening experience.

The cheapest way to ride on a bus or tram or on the metro is to buy a *strippenkaart* (strips ticket) from post offices, newsagents, tobacconists, train stations, supermarkets or VVV offices. This ticket consists of a number of individual *strippen* (strips); the more strips you buy at one time, the cheaper your travel is.

There are also machines that sell strips but the instructions are in Dutch only. For a newcomer, this whole process seems quite complicated – figuring precisely how many strips you will need for a given journey through several zones is not an easy matter. But rather than going into all the technical details here, it is easier to ask a Dutch friend or colleague to explain them to you once you get to the Netherlands. Your local transport office can also give you a multi-language brochure.

The good news is that for short trips (2-8 *strippen)* you can also pay the bus or tram driver directly, even though this is more expensive than using a *strippenkaart*. In any case, however, to be valid (and to prevent you from having to pay a fine) your tickets must be validated at the beginning of every trip, either by a ticket-stamping machine or by the bus or tram driver if he or she sells you the tickets.

## *Bicycles*

Cycling is such an important part of Dutch life that it is worth discussing in some detail.

If you already have a bike, by all means bring it with you. If you do not, even if you do not normally ride a bicycle you should consider buying one (or for day use, renting one) as soon as possible after your arrival.

*Bicycles are used by Dutch people of all ages.*

The reason is that because the Netherlands is so flat, so small, so congested and has such good bike lanes, a bicycle is a very practical aid to daily life. They are widely used by men and women (young and old alike) and by teenagers and children. Typical uses are commuting to work or school, shopping (most bikes have two big panniers for groceries and many have seats for small children as well) and day or overnight recreational trips.

There is roughly one bicycle for each of the nearly 16 million inhabitants of the country. The Dutch have built a unique and very dense network of about 19,200 km (11,930 miles) of separate bicycle lanes. These keep bicycles and cars apart, making cycling much safer and certainly much less stressful than it is in other countries.

This network is clearly marked with the ANWB's red and white signs and mushroom-shaped posts, which give the quickest bicycle route from one point to another. Bike paths are also marked by special safety signs, which must be obeyed. For example, a white bicycle on a round blue sign means that both regular bicycles *(fietsen)* and mopeds *(bromfietsen)* may use that lane. On the other hand, a rectangular sign marked *Fietspad* (bicycle path) indicates that only bicycles (not mopeds) are allowed there.

The sign *Fietsers oversteken* ("bicyclists cross here") means that the bike path is about to cross a road used by cars and that both cyclists and motorists must be especially careful. Drivers must at all times watch with the utmost care for bikes being ridden by children or teenagers. Even though these young people may make sudden unpredictable manoeuvres, they will probably still have the legal right of way.

Dutch bikes and bike shops are of excellent quality. Helmets are not required but all bicycles should have safe handlebars, front and rear lights that work, a functioning bell and a rear mudguard. Most Dutch bicycles come equipped with a built-in lock which secures the rear wheel but given the very high rate of bike thefts, a heavy chain with a separate lock is a prudent investment. Bike insurance is a good idea too, especially for a new machine.

127

Bicycles can also be hired for day use in many places in the Netherlands, e.g., at 150 railway stations. Most of these will be workhorse machines with only one gear. This will be sufficient for city use but if you are riding any distance, peddling into the wind or carrying anything heavier than a rain suit, you will find that three gears are very welcome. So if you do buy a bike of your own, make sure it has at least three gears.

*A fine mahogany pleasure launch – a joy to behold and a great way to see the country.*

## *Travel by Water*

Travel by water is one of the best ways to get to the Netherlands and to enjoy it once you are there. The major ferry ports are Vlissingen, Rotterdam and Hook of Holland *(Hoek van Holland)*, with many crossings from and to the UK. You can also travel underwater to and from the UK– by train, with or without your car – via the Channel Tunnel.

The English word "yacht" comes from the Dutch *jacht* and it should come as no surprise that the Dutch love being out on the water. Sailing craft and motor yachts of various shapes and sizes are readily available for sale or rent in the Netherlands.

Many boats for rent have an official one-to-five star classification indicating the facilities they offer. Historic Dutch ships with a great deal of character, most of them flat-bottomed boats skippered by a professional captain, can also be hired. These include the colourful *tjalken* (spritsail barges), *botters* (fishing smacks), schooners and clippers. Motorized, luxuriously converted cargo vessels known as Dutch barges – usually big, narrow, heavy steel boats from 30 to 50 metres long with the pilot house set far astern– can also be engaged for group charters.

You can take boat trips on Dutch canals, lakes (IJsselmeer) and rivers (Rhine, Maas, Waal and Eastern Scheldt). Excellent boat tours of the port of Rotterdam are offered by the SPIDO company. Its day-long *Deltawerken en zeven rivieren* (Delta Works and seven rivers) trip is also recommended.

## *DOCUMENTS NEEDED*

As a foreigner, obtaining all the necessary paperwork and keeping it in good order is important in any country. The Netherlands is certainly no exception. Indeed, the Dutch are very fond of rules, regulations and red tape – as you will soon find out.

## *Visa*

As a general rule, citizens from EU countries, the US or from certain other countries who are coming to the Netherlands as tourists do not need visas for a stay of up to three months. A valid passport or a valid identity card (for EU citizens) will suffice.

Because visa rules and regulations may change, however, it is essential that you check with the nearest Netherlands embassy or consulate to find out if you do need a visa or a temporary resident permit and if so how to apply for one.

### *Temporary Residence Permit*

For stays of more than three months a temporary residence permit *(machtiging tot voorlopig verblijf,* or MVV) is needed – except by EU nationals and those from certain other countries (such as: Australia, Austria, Canada, Finland, Iceland, Japan, Liechtenstein, Monaco, New Zealand, Norway, Sweden, Switzerland and the US).

Please note that if a MVV is needed, it must be applied for at the Netherlands embassy or consulate in your own country or in your country of residence.

### *Aliens Police*

If you plan to stay for more than 90 days, within eight working days after you arrive you must register personally with the Aliens Police *(Vreemdelingenpolitie)*, an office of which is usually located at the major police stations.

Check with the nearest one first to learn what supporting evidence (photos, employment documents, etc.) are needed to apply for the appropriate residence permit, of which there are several types.

### *Population Register*

You may have to go to the Population Register *(Bevolkingsregister)* at the local Town Hall *(Stadhuis)* before you go to the Aliens Police: call first.

Unless you are a national of one of the countries exempt from these procedures – check with a Netherlands embassy or consulate to find out – a vast amount of paperwork may be required by the Population Register.

This can include not only your own passport but also the rental/purchase agreement on a flat or house in the Netherlands, proof of registration if staying at a hotel, birth certificate, marriage certificate or divorce certificate.

It is essential to note that some of these documents may first have to be authenticated by an Apostille Certificate, which can usually be provided only by the municipality where the document itself was issued. If you were married in your living room in Kathmandu, Nepal – as the author of this book was – getting an Apostille Certificate can pose enormous bureaucratic challenges.

## *Social Fiscal Number*

After you have successfully navigated your way through the reefs and shoals of the Aliens Police and Population Register procedures, you must then apply for a Social Fiscal number *(SoFi)* if you will be employed in the Netherlands. Local Dutch tax authorities can advise you on how to do this.

## *Work Permit*

Unless you are an EU national, you will need a permit *(werkvergunning)* if you are going to be employed by a company in the Netherlands. This is not always easy to get: for details, see the chapter on "Doing Business in the Netherlands."

## *MONEY*

Until it is replaced by the Euro (the exchange rate will be about f2.20 to the Euro), the Dutch unit of currency is the guilder, variously abbreviated as f, Dfl or fl, all of which derive from its old name, *florin*, or as NLG (Netherlands guilder).

The guilder is a strong, stable, freely convertible currency. One hundred cents make up one guilder. Prices are rounded off to the nearest five cents, as the cent (1/100 of a guilder) is no longer in circulation. Coins are: *stuiver* (5 cents), *dubbeltje* (10 cents), *kwartje* (25 cents), *gulden* (NLG 1 or 100 cents), *rijksdaalder* (NLG 2.50) and five guilders (NLG 5). There are two commemorative coins with values of NLG 10 and NLG 50 which are also legal tender.

Current banknotes are: NLG 10, NLG 25, NLG 50, NLG 100, NLG 250 and NLG 1,000.

As their personal cheques, the Dutch use Eurocheques backed up by a Europas (a cheque guarantee card). When your Dutch bank gives you a Europas it will also give you a PIN code (Personal Identity Number). This is extremely useful to have because with it you can get guilders 24 hours a day from any automatic cash dispenser *(geldautomaat)*. The Dutch also use cash and debit and credit cards extensively.

The Dutch can pay their bills with bank/Giro forms. A company to whom you owe money may well send you an "accept giro" form which will already have printed on it your name and the amount to be paid. All you have to do is fill in your bank account number, sign this form and send it to the bank.

You can also use the Dutch Post Office to pay your bills. The *Postbank* does most of what a bank does but does not charge you for it. When you open a Postbank account you will also get Girocheques or a *Girobetaalkaart* (Giro card) to use for paying bills.

## MEDICAL CARE

The Dutch are the fastest growing and tallest people in Europe. Their high protein diet is probably responsible for this but the Netherlands' excellent medical care must play a major role, too.

Dutch doctors, nurses and other health workers are conscientious, well-trained and speak English. Hospitals and clinics are modern, well-designed, adequately staffed and carefully maintained.

Even though the population of the Netherlands is getting older (life expectancy is now about 75 for men and 81 for women) the average health of the population is still very good. The number of health-care facilities has not increased in recent years but there has been an increase in medical expenses. This is caused by higher salaries paid to medical workers and by more use being made of advanced medical equipment.

## Paying for Health Care

Fortunately, health care in the Netherlands is readily affordable thanks to the generous insurance schemes provided by firms for their employees, by the obligatory National Insurance *(Ziekenfonds)* or by private insurance companies. Employers must continue the pay of sick employees for one year. One of the few bits of bad news on the medical front is that there can be a long wait (sometimes months) for routine examinations and other non-urgent medical care.

## Get a Family Doctor

A family doctor normally is your first and essential point of contact in the case of physical or mental problems which are not medical emergencies. If necessary he or she will refer you to a specialist or to a hospital. It is therefore important that you find a family doctor and register with him or her as soon as possible after you get to the Netherlands.

Friends or neighbours can advise you on which one to choose. Alternatively, you can look in the Yellow Pages under the heading of *Artsen-huisartsen* or in the telephone directory under *huisartsen-(groeps)praktijk*.

## AIDS

Deaths from AIDS are decreasing now because people are being more careful and there is a programme to supply drug addicts with clean needles. In Amsterdam, however, AIDS is still the leading cause of death in men between the ages of 30 and 50.

## *TELECOMMUNICATIONS*

Telecommunications in Holland have taken a great leap forward recently as a result of privatization, more competition and fewer rules and regulations. There is now much more use of phones, computers and faxes.

Seven million people now have mobile telephones. Indeed these are nearly mandatory for families with teenage children (my brother-in-law's family in Zeeland, for example, has three cellphones). Dutch and foreign companies use a "call-back" system (this means that you do not necessarily use the local telephone company when making a call but the cheapest available rate – for example, a rate offered by a company overseas). In the Netherlands today, having e-mail (electronic mail) is virtually essential; people routinely have their e-mail number on their business card along with their phone and fax numbers.

### *Telephones*

The country code for the Netherlands is 31; the international access code from a Dutch telephone is 00.

The public telephone network in the Netherlands is operated by PTT Telecom. You can apply to this firm for phone and fax connections. For mobile telephones, contact either PTT Telecom or the Libertel company. Because Dutch operators are multilingual, they can easily help foreigners who want to get the number of a person or a company in the Netherlands.

One custom in the Netherlands you should be aware of: it is considered good manners to answer the phone by giving your name rather than by simply saying "hello."

### *Computers and Faxes*

Virtually all Dutch offices and many homes as well now have modern computers and faxes. There has been a spectacular increase in the number of state-of-the-art PCs (personal computers) equipped with CD-I (compact disk interactive) and CD-ROM (compact disk read-only memory) capabilities. Many Dutch households will soon have such PCs if they do not have them already.

By the year 2000, nearly half of the population will also have access, via the Dutch TV cable network, to the worldwide computer network Internet, the use of which is already growing by 10% per month. Amsterdam bills itself as "the digital city" because via the Internet you get access to its postal, press and government services. You can even go to its digital cafe to meet computer experts, participate in on-line discussion groups and play computer games.

You should consider getting plugged into the Internet yourself, if only so you can use e-mail and can contact friends and relatives around the world at a very low cost.

## *ELECTRICAL EQUIPMENT*

Because the Netherlands is on the 220 volt, 50 Hz, three-phase European system, electrical equipment built to American or other standards will require transformers. But even when so equipped, items with electric timing mechanisms or electric motors may not work very well. Audio equipment is notoriously hard to convert. European TV sets and video systems are not compatible with those used in the US.

## *LEISURE ACTIVITIES*

The Dutch have always been keen on cultural activities and sports and love to entertain at home. They will usually be happy to have you join them, too.

Today in order of their popularity the most common leisure pursuits are: watching TV; meeting friends; participating in games, hobbies and sports; going out to restaurants or for cultural activities; and reading, which is still popular but is decreasing. Volunteer work, however, is becoming more popular, especially among women.

*In winter waterways turn to ice, providing people of all ages with new opportunities to enjoy the outdoors.*

## Sports

People between the ages of 36 and 65 are becoming more and more interested in sports, especially in swimming, biking, fitness, football, tennis and golf. But perhaps because of the pressures of school, jobs or having young children, the younger generation (ages 15-35) seems be to getting somewhat less interested in sports.

In any case, as has been suggested earlier, even if you are not very athletically inclined yourself it is still a good idea for you to join a sports club in order to meet the Dutch and make some new friends.

## CULTURAL ACTIVITIES

### TV and Films

Even without the addition of a satellite dish, Dutch TV will provide a wide range of programmes in Dutch and other languages. Cable TV brings in a deluge of foreign TV programmes (English, French, Italian, German, Turkish) transmitted in their original languages. Foreign films are shown at local cinemas in their native language with Dutch subtitles (not dubbing) added.

### Plays, Opera, Dance, Music, Museums, Theme Parks

There is never a shortage of cultural activities in the big Dutch cities. Newspapers on Thursday and Friday will have information about upcoming events scheduled for the next week. Entertainment guides are also widely available. Tickets can be ordered from box offices at theatres, from VVV offices and from reservation booking offices.

VVV has a definitive list of museums in the Netherlands (there are about 1,050 of them and some are among the best in the world) and sells special "Museum cards" so that you can visit them at low cost. The trend among museums seems to be toward more mega-exhibits, such as the widely-acclaimed Vermeer exhibition of 1996.

Expatriate and Dutch children (and young-at-heart adults, too) will be glad to hear that more and more theme parks are being built in the Netherlands.

## ENTERTAINING AT HOME

At one time or another, invitations for morning coffee, for drinks before dinner, for dinner itself or for post-dinner coffee-and-snack are certain to be forthcoming: the Dutch enjoy meeting foreigners and take pride in entertaining them at home. Please see the earlier section on "Invitations and good manners" for some helpful hints.

## *RELIGION*

The Dutch Constitution guarantees freedom of religion. All the major world faiths – Christian, Muslim, Hindu, Jewish, etc. – are represented in the Netherlands, together with the many different denominations grouped under their banners.

For the last 30 years organized religion has been declining as a potent force in Dutch life. If this trend continues, within the coming generation only about 25% of the population will be members of a church.

In the meantime, however, many individual churches, temples and congregations are still quite active today. You should therefore have no difficulty finding one to your liking. In most cases, the services will be conducted in Dutch but there are some English-language services in the major cities.

## *PETS*

Many of the Dutch keep a pet. Dogs are especially popular, as a walk along any city pavement will quickly reveal. Do watch where you put your feet!

There is no quarantine for pets being imported into the Netherlands. For dogs and cats, you will need a valid health certificate (10 days old at the most), stating that the animal has been inoculated against rabies. The certificate, in Dutch, French, German or English, must also give the date of the inoculation, the type of vaccine, a description of the animal and the owner's name.

This document must be endorsed by the official veterinary department of the country of origin (except for Switzerland, Austria and the USA). The animal must have been vaccinated at least 30 days before it crosses the Dutch border.

Dog owners in the Netherlands must pay dog license fees *(hondenbelasting)*. They can apply for a license by filling out forms obtained from a post office. Failure to do so may result in a fine.

## *EMERGENCIES*

The emergency telephone number in the Netherlands is 112. By calling it you can contact the police, fire brigade or ambulance service. Be ready to explain what kind of help you need and where it is needed.

# Chapter Twelve

# DOING BUSINESS IN THE NETHERLANDS

Just as the Netherlands is a good place to live, it is also a good place to do business. The hard-working Dutch have a long tradition of being successful world traders. Their thriftiness is legendary. As an old saying has it, *op de kleintjes letten* – "watch the little ones," that is, watch the pennies and the pounds will take care of themselves. Business still is a highly respectable occupation – and so is making money.

## *NO HIDDEN SNAGS*

Business in the Netherlands is conducted aboveboard and in a straightforward way. The Dutch put a very high value on integrity, efficiency, directness and honesty. A Dutch business partner – and it is a good idea of have one if you are setting up a sizeable enterprise – is not likely to cheat you. There is virtually no official corruption. The governmental, tax and legal systems of the Netherlands can be complicated and very frustrating but at least they are not malevolent, on the take or staffed by incompetents.

To be able to take full advantage of the business opportunities available today, it may first be useful to learn a bit about the Dutch economy and work force, about working in the Netherlands and about Dutch business manners, taxes, opening hours and holidays.

The information in this chapter will let you hold your own intellectually in any gathering of the Dutch business world. But you will find it has practical applications, too, no matter whether you are an employee of a multinational company in Rotterdam or whether you decide to go to work for yourself as a freelance consultant. Most importantly, it may also give you some ideas about where your own talents can be put to best use.

## LEARNING ABOUT DUTCH BUSINESS LIFE

The World Trade Institute, which is part of the Beurs-World Trade Center in Rotterdam, offers an evening introductory course (in English and for a fee) on Dutch business life. Although this is designed primarily for foreign entrepreneurs who are setting up a business in the Netherlands, it may interest freelance workers too, because it covers so much useful ground.

The course looks at the organizational structure of the Netherlands, market research and market information, international trade, permits and liability, the financial system of the Netherlands, employees and work contracts, taxation and duty, and living and working in the Rotterdam area. Less ambitious "customized" courses, tailored to your own specific needs, can also be arranged.

## THE DUTCH ECONOMY: AN OVERVIEW

To do business in any country you should know what makes its economy tick. Fortunately, by using only two sonorous words – one English and the other Dutch – we can try to sum up the economy of the Netherlands in the year 2000.

The first word is globalization, which means that the Dutch now treat the whole world as a single unified market for their goods, services and ideas.

The second word is *econologie*, which is a composite of the Dutch words for "economy" and "ecology." This means that the Dutch realize that *economic growth*, on the one hand, and *protecting the environment*, on the other, must be taken into account simultaneously because they are but two sides of the same coin.

What we are saying, then, is that the modern Dutch economy not only has a global reach but has also embraced the idea that more economic growth should not automatically mean more harm to the environment. Since business opportunities may exist in international trade and environmental matters alike, let us look briefly at both of them.

## GLOBALIZATION

### Major Dutch Companies

Dutch companies have done well. *Fortune* magazine's annual list of the 500 biggest companies includes a goodly number of Dutch firms involved in world trade. A partial list would include: Shell (petroleum), Unilever (a wide range of goods, from ice creams to soaps), Philips (electronics), ABN-AMRO (banking), ING (banking), Ahold (food) and Akzo (chemicals).

Because of its global reach, the Dutch economy has always been extremely sensitive to fluctuations in the value of the currencies of its trading partners. A good example is Fokker, the famous Dutch aviation company. To manufacture its high quality aircraft, Fokker had to pay for raw materials, supplies and component parts with expensive Dutch guilders and German marks. The finished aircraft, however, were sold for US dollars. When the dollar dropped sharply, Fokker could not pay its creditors and had to declare bankruptcy.

On a more positive note, potential investors may be pleased to learn that the Amsterdam stock exchange – the oldest in the world – is still one of the top 10 international securities markets today.

## *Depending on World Trade*

The Netherlands depends on world trade because it is primarily an exporting nation. It is number 7 of the top 10 exporting countries (after the US, Germany, Japan, France, UK and Italy). Dutch exports are almost 4% of the world's total exports. About 75-80% of these exports go to other EU countries, of which Germany by far the biggest market, taking 25% of them.

This heavy reliance on foreign trade is both a weakness and a strength for the Netherlands.

It is a weakness because Dutch analysts believe the focal point of the global economy is now shifting away from Western Europe and therefore away from the Netherlands itself. Asia has been strong in the past few years; Latin America and Eastern Europe may be waiting in the wings for their turn on the world's economic stage tomorrow. If so, the lower labour costs of these countries could eventually result in more unemployment in the Netherlands, where wages are much higher.

Another weakness is that world exports are now growing most rapidly in fields which are not Dutch specialties – for example, state-of-the-art electronics. (Philips does make high technology electronic products but these are usually manufactured in Asia, not in the Netherlands itself.)

At the same time, however, foreign trade is also a strong point for the Netherlands.

Many of the traditional Dutch exports – machinery, textiles, agricultural produce, petroleum products, chemicals and metals – do not require extraordinarily advanced technology to produce. But the Dutch manage to turn out these relatively low-tech goods so efficiently, in such high volume and with such good quality that they can still compete in foreign markets. And as the Asian, Latin American and Eastern European economies get stronger they will also offer new markets for Dutch goods and services.

## *FOREIGN INVESTMENT IS WELCOME*

The Netherlands Foreign Investment Agency can tick off some persuasive reasons why foreign companies like to set up shop in the Netherlands: it has the perfect infrastructure, a healthy business environment with tax treaties with more than 50 countries around the world, a stable economic and political climate, and a high quality of life.

Not surprisingly, direct foreign investment has increased rapidly – American, Swiss, Belgian, Japanese companies like to invest in the Netherlands. It is also a favourite site for companies' European headquarters and for their distribution and logistics centres.

In one recent year, for example, 35% of all the company headquarters newly established in Europe were placed in the Netherlands. Such prominent firms as Eastman Chemicals, KPMG, Nalco, Sybase, Intergraph, Canon, Mitsubishi Motors, Nissan and Mita all have their European headquarters in the Netherlands.

In addition, nearly half of the US companies and more than 40% of the Japanese companies which have established a European distribution centre (EDC) have decided to put their EDCs in the Netherlands. Examples of these firms are Canon, Digital Equipment, IBM, Okda, Nissan, Omron, Polaroid, Rank Xerox, Sony, and Unisys.

Other foreign companies – Apple Computer, Packard Bell, Hewlett Packard, and Outukumpu Steel, to name a few of them – have chosen the Netherlands as the site for their "value-added logistics centres," which specialize in product assembly, repackaging, quality control and repair.

About 6,800 foreign companies, large and small, have set up their European operations in the Netherlands. More than 380,000 people – the vast majority of them Dutch – now work for or with these foreign companies.

## *OLD BARRIERS ARE COMING DOWN*

One result of globalization is that the old, well-established national and physical barriers are beginning to crumble.

In the Netherlands itself, *internationalism* is the order of the day. The Dutch are pushing hard for the further unification of Europe; already nearly half of their recent laws are a direct result of EU legislation. Dutch trading houses are looking beyond the domestic market and are becoming international distributors. Dutch transporters (mainly truckers but also ship owners) are handling 25% of all the cross-border transport in Europe.

Physically, the Randstad, the most densely populated part of the Netherlands, is moving in a direction which has aptly been called "post-urban California." This means that its four big cities (Amsterdam, Rotterdam, The Hague and Utrecht) will no longer be separate physical units but will become, much like southern California, an ever-shifting river of people, information, money and goods with no barriers between living, play and work areas.

In fact, the only Dutch enterprises which are still inextricably tied to a given location are the heavy industries, harbour and airline companies. The one thing that other firms need is road access to their customers. In fact, some companies do not even need this. A new communications business like Libertel (which handles mobile telephones), for example, sees nothing wrong in setting up shop in Limburg, which is located as far away from the Randstad as possible – in the southernmost tip of the Netherlands.

## *ECONOLOGIE: ECONOMIC GROWTH WITH MINIMAL POLLUTION*

With their usual caution, Dutch businessmen might say that the economy "is not doing badly." In fact it is doing quite well now – even better than expected. Compared to other European states, the Netherlands has had an excellent growth rate. In 1999, for example, the economy rose by 3.7%, while inflation fell below 2% and unemployment declined to 2.6%.

Most importantly, economic progress and protecting the environment now go hand-in-hand. Prosperity no longer means economic quantity alone: it is understood to be a qualitative matter closely connected to the health of the environment.

The modern Dutch vocabulary is therefore studded with words like "econologie," "ecotax," "manure bookkeeping" and "sustainable growth." The government itself has become very actively involved in environmental issues and they have become an important and permanent part of the national budget.

While living in the Netherlands you will find that Dutch companies are now very "eco-conscious" and that industries are working on new ways to get rid of wastes, recycle materials and produce goods more efficiently. In fact, they have succeeded to the extent that Dutch environmental expertise has now become an export product in its own right.

## *THE DUTCH WORK FORCE*

The president of a foreign computer software company put it in a nutshell. At the upper end of the employment scale, he said, "we found that the Netherlands offers the most sophisticated talent pool in Europe." The high degree of job competence in the Netherlands is largely the result of the country's excellent educational system and is perhaps the most important single reason the Dutch economy is performing so well in global competition.

The Dutch also have the most flexible workforce in Western Europe. There are, for example, more than 700,000 flexi-workers – men and women who work within a variable number of hours or who are on a temporary contract for less than one year. This is 10% of the total workforce and if we add to it the large number of small tradesmen and other self-employed people, the total number of flexi-workers turns out to be 1.2 million, i.e., about 20% of the work force.

These flexi-workers play a vital role in the Dutch economy by filling temporary gaps in production and service industries. This is important because in the Netherlands it is extremely difficult for management to fire anyone or to tamper with the regular work week.

But the lot of the flexi-workers is not always an enviable one. Many of them are school dropouts or immigrants. They have only limited prospects, less security than people on long term contracts, no higher education, do not earn much money, have no pension buildup, no early retirement, no additional on-the-job training and no company-financed insurance against illness, disability or unemployment.

Moreover, the Dutch economy is shifting away from heavy industry (which in any case is becoming more automated and needs fewer workers) and toward the service industries. There will therefore be fewer low-level industrial, commercial and administrative jobs.

Instead, the demand will be for talented, highly-trained men and women – for example, computer programmers, systems analysts, managers, journalists, interpreters, international lawyers, logistics experts, artists, and people in the medical and semi-medical professions.

If you happen to fall into one of these "in-demand" job categories and if you learn Dutch you may well be able to find work in the Netherlands. But see below first!

## WORKING IN THE NETHERLANDS

### Work Permits

EU nationals do not need a Dutch work permit (commonly known as a *werkvergunning)* and can take any job they can get. But if you are not an EU national and if you want to work for any company in the Netherlands, whether as a shop assistant or as the Chief Executive Officer, you will have to get a work permit from the labour exchange *(Arbeidsbureau)* in the city of your proposed employment.

It takes some effort for expatriates to get work permits. The basic problem is that the Dutch will not issue them except to people who have special skills which are not available either in the Netherlands or in the wider EU workforce.

The Dutch workforce itself is so well-trained and so flexible that it can usually supply whatever skills are needed. Other problems are that the employer as well as the employee must apply for the work permit and that many employers want their workers to know Dutch. Furthermore, a foreigner who hopes to be officially transferred to the Netherlands by his or her employer abroad must have worked for that employer for at least one year.

## *Working on Your Own*

The good news is that you do not need a work permit to work freelance. So if you have a skill which is in demand, you may be able to become a freelance consultant. Being able to speak and read Dutch will of course be an enormous asset but you may be able to get by without this skill if you have a product that is wanted badly enough.

Nor in most cases do you need a work permit to start your own small business. A business permit, however, will probably be needed for entrepreneurs who want to engage in certain endeavours in Rotterdam or other big cities.

Examples of such urban enterprises are: itinerant trade (market and street trade), second-hand trade, retail trade (opening a shop), skilled trades (e.g., house painters), catering, and some service companies (e.g., operating a beauty salon).

Otherwise, if there is something you can make and sell yourself, it is easy enough to set up your own business: the main thing you need is a listing with the local Chamber of Commerce *(Kamer van Koophandel)*, which is also an excellent source of information on business permits and commercial prospects in general.

## *Hiring and Firing*

If you do set up your own business, however, please be careful before you hire any employees: it is very hard to get rid of them. In theory, instant dismissal can be justified when an employee is truly incompetent, steals from you, grossly neglects his or her duty or repeatedly refuses to follow reasonable instructions. In practice, however, any employee so dismissed will immediately seek legal redress and you may find yourself involved in an long, expensive legal battle.

## *Childcare*

Because relatively few Dutch mothers have full-time jobs, the Netherlands does not offer the newcomer a wide range of child care facilities available in other countries.

If you have very young children (under the age of five) it may be difficult to find someone to look after them. So unless you can somehow manage to work out of your own home until the children are old enough to go to school, this can severely limit your employment prospects.

## *Employment Contracts*

Legally, if you work full-time for someone who has the right to give you instructions which you must follow, you are considered to be an employee. The means you will need an employment contract.

Such contracts can be made verbally or in writing but to avoid any possible misunderstandings and legal battles it is much better to have a formal written contract signed by both the employer and the employee.

Salaries are negotiable and are usually paid each month into your giro or bank account. However, because of the very heavy tax burden (see below) your net pay may well be about half of your gross earnings. So other benefits (some of them taxable, too) are frequently offered by employers to recruit and keep good employees.

Perhaps you may be able to negotiate some of these attractive "extras" into your own work contract: one additional month of pay each year (this is referred to as "the 13th month"); rewards for high productivity; commissions on sales; profit-sharing arrangements; access to company canteens or social clubs; help with savings, mortgages or pensions; a company car; and allowances for business expenses.

## *TAXES*

The high quality of life in the Netherlands has to be paid for somehow and as a result the Dutch are one of the most heavily-taxed peoples in the world. Tax rates vary with income level and range from a low of 33% to a high of 60%. If you are transferred by your company to the Netherlands or if you work there in some other capacity you, too, will be liable to these stiff taxes.

But because the tax picture is always subject to change and is quite complicated (for example, there is a special – and very favourable – expatriate tax status technically known as the "35% ruling" which may apply to you), it is strongly recommend that you seek qualified tax advice once you are in the Netherlands.

Friends or colleagues may well know someone in this business. Tax consultants are also listed in the Yellow Pages under the heading *Belasting consulenten/belasting adviseurs* or in the telephone directory under *belastingadviesburo*.

As a first step, however, two booklets in English are excellent sources of tax and other useful information for expatriates: "Living and Working in the Netherlands," co-authored by KPMG International Business Support and Formula Two Relocations (Amsterdam), and "Foreign nationals working in the Netherlands," produced by the accounting firm of Coopers & Lybrand (Amsterdam).

These booklets will explain that as a general rule you will have to pay withholding tax (also known as wage tax) and personal income tax. You will certainly have to pay municipal taxes and may be subject to other taxes as well – for example, net wealth tax, real estate tax, and inheritance and gift tax. Finally, in most cases you will also have to contribute to the Dutch social security system.

TRIGG

## *BUSINESS MANNERS*

The Dutch are direct, open people and not given to Machiavellian intrigues. They will undoubtedly excuse any minor social blunders you may make but just to be on the safe side here are seven helpful hints on Dutch business etiquette.

1. **Be honest and modest.** Because the Netherlands scores very highly on comparative scales of international business integrity, it is extremely important that expatriate businessmen and businesswomen be perceived, above all, as being honest. Toward this end, until you can form some clear idea of what the acceptable limits of exaggeration are, you should limit yourself to describing your products and your own achievements only in the most accurate and most modest terms.

2. **Don't be too informal.** Using someone's first name without being asked to do so is considered very impolite. Business cards are extremely useful to get names and titles right. "Drs.", for example, signifies a university graduate, not a medical doctor or a Ph.D., which is abbreviated as "Dr."

3. **Remember that the Dutch are very busy people.** Making appointments well in advance of a proposed meeting is essential: turning up uninvited or asking for an appointment on very short notice suggests a lack of consideration. Always be on time and never take up more time than is actually needed to conduct your business.

4. **Don't count on working lunches.** Most people have only 45 minutes or so in which to have a sandwich or a quick snack for lunch. The long working lunch, replete with food and drink at a good restaurant and hopefully culminating in a deal, is not as common in the Netherlands as in the US or UK.

5. **Don't forget about birthdays.** As mentioned in the chapter on "Dutch Customs," birthdays are important events. When it is your

151

own birthday you must bring cakes to the office so that during a coffee break your colleagues can celebrate this happy occasion.

6. **Finish your business during normal working hours.** The official work week is 36 hours and for most people this is enough. A Dutch man or woman usually wants to be home for dinner by about 6:30 p.m., which means they have to leave the office relatively early, given the inevitable commute involved. Working business dinners are occasionally arranged, however, either to continue discussions about unresolved issues or (more likely) to celebrate a deal, but they will rarely begin later than 7:00 p.m.

7. **Join a business club.** In the big Dutch cities there is no shortage of international and bilateral business clubs, Rotary organizations or international Chambers of Commerce to choose from. By joining one or more of these organizations you will not only make useful business contacts but will also get a chance to see Dutch business manners in action.

## *OPENING HOURS*

Normal shopping hours are Monday through Friday from 8:30/9:00 a.m. to 5:30/6:00 p.m. and Saturday from 8:30/9:00 a.m. to 4:00/5:00 p.m. Many shops are allowed to stay open seven days a week until 8:00 p.m. or 10:00 p.m. More and more shops and supermarkets open on Sundays from noon to 5:00 p.m.

Most shops close for one morning, one afternoon or one whole day each week; a sign in the window will give specific times. Many do not open until 1:00 p.m. on Monday but offer late-night shopping on Thursday or Friday evenings until 9:00 p.m. Some shops close for lunch. Most Dutch towns have a market once a week.

Business hours are Monday through Friday from 8:30 a.m. to 5:00 p.m.

Banks are open Monday through Friday from 9:00 a.m. to 4:00/ 5:00 p.m. and usually on one evening, too, to coincide with late-night shopping.

The hours of government offices are Monday through Friday from 8:00/8:30 a.m. to 5:00 p.m.

Supermarkets are generally open from 8:00 a.m. - 8:00 p.m.

Chemists (pharmacies) are open Monday to Friday from 8:00/9:00 a.m. to 5:30 p.m. Some chemists will always be open (in rotation) to cover evening, night and weekend needs.

Restaurant hours vary but restaurants are usually open for lunch from 11:00 a.m. to 2:30/3:00 p.m. and for dinner from 5:30 to 10:00 p.m. The Dutch like to eat dinner relatively early, so do not expect to be served if you turn up at 10:00 p.m.

## HOLIDAYS AND OTHER NATIONAL CELEBRATIONS

When no dates are given, this means the holiday or celebration is held on a varying schedule.

- **December 31 - January 1:** New Year's Eve is celebrated with loud firecrackers and fireworks before, at and after midnight. One of the most traditional foods of this season is *oliebollen* ("oil balls" – round sugared donuts filled with raisins). New Year's Day is a public holiday.

- **March/April:** Some shops and offices close on Good Friday. Easter Monday is a public holiday.

- **April 30:** *Koninginnedag*, the birthday of Queen Juliana, is still celebrated as the Queen's official birthday and is a public holiday. Queen Beatrix goes to one or two towns on this festive occasion and is greeted with parades, flags and music.

- **May 4:** Memorial Day commemorates those who died in World War II. It is not an official holiday but at 8:00 p.m. two minutes of silence are observed.

- **May 5:** Liberation Day celebrates the liberation of the Netherlands by Allied armies in 1945. This is a public holiday only once every five years.

153

- **May:** Ascension Day is a public holiday.
- **May/June:** Whit Monday is also a public holiday.
- **June:** Performing artists from all over the world come to the Netherlands for the annual Holland Festival, which features theatre, dance and music.
- **September:** The third Tuesday of September is Prinsjesdag (Prince's Day), when the Queen, arriving majestically in her golden coach, officially opens the next session of Parliament.
- **December 5:** *Sinterklaas* celebrations in the evening (see the chapter on "Dutch Customs").
- **December 25 – 26:** Christmas Day and Boxing Day are both public holidays. In the past, no major presents were given on Christmas Day. Instead, families and friends met for lunch or dinner and went to church together. Gradually, however, the Dutch are beginning to follow the tradition of giving each other presents on Christmas instead of at Sinterklaas.

# Chapter Thirteen

# PROSPECTS FOR THE FUTURE

Forecasting is a hazardous calling at best but the Netherlands' overall prospects for the future seem to be quite good. The quality of life there should remain one of the highest in the world. At least four issues, however – immigrants and asylum seekers, jobs, the "greying" (ageing) of the population, and shifts in popular attitudes – will require some creative solutions.

## IMMIGRANTS AND ASYLUM SEEKERS

Immigrants, and to a lesser extent asylum seekers, are a taboo subject in the Netherlands, where it is extremely important always to be politically-correct on ethnic issues. The Dutch phrase for such a sensitive issue is *heet hangijzer*, "a hot pothanger" – equivalent to the American expression "a hot potato." Indeed, it took the crash of an El

Al cargo plane in 1992 (the plane went down in the Bijlmermeer, a neighbourhood on the outskirts of Amsterdam where many illegal immigrants live) to bring this subject out into the open, at least temporarily.

When they get to know you well, the ethnic Dutch will probably share with you their opinions on immigrants and asylum seekers, whether these views are positive, negative or a little bit of both. If so, you will find it useful to have some factual background information on this issue. Because it has become one of the most important topics on the Dutch political agenda, it is worth going into at some length.

## *More and More Immigrants*

Tensions between the immigrants (referred to by the Dutch as *allochtonen*, literally, "other-landers") and the ethnic Dutch are not getting any worse, so this is not a potentially explosive situation at present. But as in many other western European countries, the problem of immigrants will continue to defy easy solution.

In recent years there has been a high immigration rate: over 70,000 people came to the Netherlands in 1999 to be reunited with their families. Although family reunion immigration is expected to decrease somewhat as immigrants find marriage partners among the other immigrants in the Netherlands rather than in their native countries, there is also an influx of Europeans from other European countries.

The bottom line is that now more than 2.7 million people (17.2% of the total population) are of non-Dutch origin. Of this number, 1.3 million are of non-Western origin. As the immigrant population grows, nearly half of the population in the Netherlands' largest cities will consist of immigrants and many neighborhoods in these cities will have clear immigrant majorities.

## *The Three Generations*

After an initial influx of foreign workers from Italy and Spain in the 1960s, the first generation of immigrants came from Morocco, Turkey or Suriname and kept many of their old traditions.

Their children, now referred to as the second generation of immigrants, received part or all of their education in Dutch schools and can therefore speak and write understandable if not always flawless Dutch. At home, however, their parents may insist that they speak the parental language and that they follow highly conservative customs.

What police and social welfare officials hope is that the children of these children (i.e., the third generation of immigrants) will be more fully integrated into Dutch life. Many ethnic Dutch, however, fear that the process of assimilation may take several more generations – or, indeed, that it may never occur at all.

## *The Slow Pace of Assimilation*

Three factors are slowing this process now. The first is that not all immigrants want their children to become carbon copies of the Dutch. They sometimes send the children to highly conservative religious (usually Islamic) schools, a step which tends to isolate them from the broader currents of secular Dutch life.

In the Netherlands, if you have 200 – or in the big cities, 300 – students you can set up a school based on a philosophical principle of your own. There are therefore Islamic schools, Hindu schools, Jewish schools, etc.

The second factor is that immigrant children tend not to do as well as ethnic Dutch children in school. Most of the immigrants have congregated in the big cities. Immigrant pupils are already the majority in Amsterdam; Rotterdam is not far behind. Although government and city officials are trying to improve matters (for example, by smaller classes), immigrant students generally fall behind ethnic Dutch students beginning in the primary school years.

157

This downward trend continues in the big cities' secondary schools, where the exit rate (students leaving school at the age of 16) is three times higher than in smaller towns. School-leavers, many of them immigrants, have only minimal qualifications and will probably have trouble finding a permanent full-time job with any prospects for advancement.

The third factor is that despite the Dutch tradition of tolerance there is in fact some racial discrimination against immigrants. Obviously feeling very guilty about having any prejudices whatsoever, the Dutch allude to these negative feelings only with close friends, sometimes in guardedly humorous terms.

## Immigrants and Crime

Unfortunately, such politically-incorrect humour does have a basis in fact because half of the prison population is of foreign extraction.

Reliable and up-to-date statistics are not available but it is clear that Moroccan immigrants have been the most likely to be in trouble with the police. A report by the Netherlands Ministry of the Interior showed that in the 1980s six times more Moroccan intercity youths aged 9 to 17 were arrested than ethnic Dutch youths. By 1992 only four times as many Moroccan youths were being arrested but in that same year one in four Moroccan boys between the ages of 12 and 17 was in contact with the police as a suspect in a theft or burglary case.

The Turkish and Surinamese have fared a bit better. In 1988 three times as many Turkish and Suriname youths were arrested compared to the ethnic Dutch but by 1992 there was little difference in their respective arrest rates. In 1992 one in six Turkish and Surinamese boys were being treated as suspects, compared to one in twenty ethnic Dutch youths.

## Inner City Problems

A number of interrelated factors are thought to contribute to immigrant crime rates. These include the stresses of inner city living, reduced levels of social control within immigrant groups themselves, minimal levels of education, low incomes, high unemployment and poor prospects for the future. The lack of jobs, however, is undoubtedly the most serious problem.

Moroccans and Turks are four to five times more likely to be unemployed than the ethnic Dutch; people from Suriname and the Antilles are twice as likely to be jobless as the ethnic Dutch. Moroccans and Turks have not been able to move into service industries as easily as Surinamese, who are native speakers of Dutch and come from a Dutch colonial background.

The high levels of immigrant unemployment in the big Dutch cities are likely to persist. Fewer unskilled workers are now needed by Dutch industry. Work itself has shifted to the outer areas of the major cities. There are more and more city people who lack marketable skills. About 50% of the jobs in major cities are now held by commuters, most of them ethnically Dutch.

## *Asylum Seekers*

For a very long time the Netherlands has been a sure place of refuge for people fleeing from political or religious persecution in their native lands or those caught up in civil or transborder wars and collapsing regimes.

After reaching the Netherlands, however, asylum seekers today face most of the same obstacles that the immigrants face. Asylum seekers have been no more successful than immigrants in coping with them, except that the asylum seekers are less likely to find themselves in trouble with the police.

Dutch asylum laws are being tightened. In 1994, for example, 52,000 people applied for asylum and 20,000 were accepted; in 1995, 29,000 applied and 19,000 were accepted. As upheavals continue in the rest of the world, this flow of desperate people from many different countries will continue to be a permanent feature of Dutch life.

## *JOBS*

The Netherlands is now a post-industrial society: only 23% of the jobs today are still in industry. The remaining 77% are in commerce, communications, services, government, education, health care, and agriculture. More and more of these "post-industrial jobs" are being created but at the same time more and more people want to work. The Netherlands must therefore maintain a high rate of economic growth (about 3% per year) to absorb new workers and at the same time begin to reduce existing unemployment.

Forecasts of the employment outlook present a mixed picture. On the one hand, more people are entering the work force. On the other, the Dutch population is ageing now (see below) and within a decade a large number of older workers will retire. It is hoped in the years ahead that the number of job seekers and of job vacancies will be roughly in balance.

On the other hand, however, many of the new entrants into the labour market will be women looking for work after they have raised their children. This may mean more splitting up of jobs and less full-time work. At the same time, young people looking for their first job will be more highly educated and may have to accept jobs which are below the level of their education.

## *THE "GREYING" OF THE POPULATION*

The Dutch population is getting older and living to a riper old age. Fourteen percent of the people are now above the age of 65. The number of older persons is rising while the number of young people is falling.

This means that the number of old age pensioners will double (to more than four million) over the next 30 years. In less than half that time, the total amounts of pensions and social benefits which must be paid to them will increase by at least 25%.

Who will pay for this? Right now there seems to be only one answer: the declining number of younger workers. So unless pensions and benefits are reduced (which is unlikely due to the political influence wielded by the older generation) these young workers may be faced with even heavier taxes.

## *SHIFTS IN POPULAR ATTITUDES*

The chattering classes of the Netherlands may be favourably impressed if you can lace your conversations with learned references to "end of century pessimism," "the lack of purpose among Dutch intellectuals" and "a new 'pillarization' based on bourgeois, popular and intellectual pillars." What is certain, however, is that Dutch attitudes toward life are now changing.

More so than other European countries, the Netherlands is becoming a purely secular society, where people join voluntary or ideological organizations strictly on the basis of their personal convictions.

There continues to be a pronounced loss of faith in organized religion as the Dutch look more and more to the private domain (their own home, family and friends) to find meaning and happiness.

There is less faith, too, in traditional childbearing: in the last 10 years the percentage of women without children has increased from 10 to 20%.

Perhaps most important in the long run is that traditional Dutch attitudes toward work are changing, too. Because their social services are so good and more people have two incomes, rather than working longer hours the Dutch increasingly want to have more free time to enjoy the good things of life.

If this trend continues, the days of the Calvinist tradition of hard work and deferred desires may at last be drawing to a close in the Netherlands. What might then take its place? My own guess, for what it is worth, is that the "pleasure-before-work" philosophy of post-urban California will have many more adherents.

# CULTURAL QUIZ

## *SITUATION ONE*

This is the first night you have spent in your newly-rented flat in a trendy neighbourhood of Amsterdam, shortly after your arrival in the Netherlands. You have an important meeting the next day and are looking forward to a good night's sleep.

The young tenants of the flat above you, however, are hosting a party to celebrate the ethnic diversity of the Netherlands. Each guest must perform a dance of his or her native land, to the rhythm of authentic music prerecorded on tape. Although you have already knocked on their door and asked the tenants to make less noise, at 3:30 a.m. the party is still going strong. You:

- **A** Resolve to speak sternly to the tenants the next day, asking them to be more considerate of the other people in the building.
- **B** Call the police.
- **C** Try to ignore the racket and get what rest you can.
- **D** Knock on their door again and ask if you can join the party and do a dance from your own country.

## *Comment*

Answer C is correct for a newcomer. If you had lived in the building for some time and had several other problems with the tenants, Answer B would be better. Calling the police at this early stage, however, would permanently alienate the tenants, who might otherwise turn out to be friendly and helpful. Speaking sternly to them would probably not result in quieter parties. Without the benefit of musical accompaniment your own native dance would probably not be a great success.

## *SITUATION TWO*

You are an international business executive. Your Dutch boss has invited you to come to his house "at about eight o'clock" on a given evening. This is the first invitation you have received in the Netherlands. You hear from colleagues in the office that both the boss and his wife greatly value their privacy at home. You:

**A** Are sure this must be an invitation for a cocktail party. (At your last foreign post, dinner was never eaten before 11:30 p.m.)

**B** Believe this is an invitation for a formal dinner. (In your home country, dinner is always served between just before 8:00 p.m.)

**C** Realize that this is an invitation for dessert after dinner. (Your own spouse often entertains friends this way at home after 8:00 p.m.)

**D** Decide, at the risk of making a grave social blunder, to telephone the wife of the boss at home to find out just what this invitation means.

## *Comment*

Answer D is correct. Since the Dutch usually eat dinner relatively early (around 6:30-7:00 p.m.) an invitation for 8:00 p.m. means coffee and biscuits, perhaps followed by drinks and a light snack. If there is any doubt in your mind about what the hostess has planned, you should certainly call her – but be sure not to give her the impression that you expect dinner.

## SITUATION THREE

While having dinner at a neighbour's house, you notice that his three young children are giggling at you and whispering to each other in Dutch. They seem to find your table manners very funny, especially your habit of eating with your fork held in your right hand. You:

   **A** Frown severely and wag your finger at the children so they will stop poking fun at you.
   **B** Practice holding the fork in your left hand for the remainder of the meal.
   **C** Request that the parents discipline their rowdy children.
   **D** Continue to hold the fork in your right hand but ask the parents to explain to the children that in your own country it is considered bad manners to eat with the fork in the left hand!

## Comment

Answer D is correct. Let the parents decide whether discipline is necessary. If you have always held a fork in your right hand, shifting it to the other hand in the middle of dinner is going to be awkward at best.

## SITUATION FOUR

You are a foreign businessman. At a cocktail party you see a pretty, vivacious Dutch lady who is the wife of one of your Dutch colleagues. You have met her socially several times before and each time you got along well and had a nice chat. She recognizes you as you approach her. You:

**A** Shake hands with her because to do anything else might be misconstrued by the lady herself or by her husband.

**B** Kiss her lightly on each cheek.

**C** Do nothing because you can't decide what to do.

## Comment

Answer B is correct. Dutch men greet their women friends, and Dutch women greet each other, by a light kiss on each cheek. A third kiss can be added for close friends.

## SITUATION FIVE

Before moving to the Netherlands, you spent some years in a country where the royal family was famous for its ostentatious standard of living and for its frequent involvement in scandals. As a result, you have very strong views on this subject. At a coffee break at the office, a Dutch colleague asks you what you think about the Dutch monarchy. You:

**A** Tell him you believe monarchies have no place in modern democracies and that not a guilder of public funds should be used to support them.

**B** Praise the selfless dedication of the Dutch House of Orange, its importance as a symbol of national unity and its tradition of keeping a low public profile.

**C** Say that you actually know very little about the House of Orange and ask your colleague to enlighten you.

## Comment

Answer C is correct. The Dutch are not highly nationalistic but as a guest you should never criticize their country and especially not the royal family, which is universally admired and respected. On the other hand, if you really are a fervent anti-monarchist you should not go out of your way to praise the Dutch monarchy.

# FURTHER READING

Much of what has been written in English about the Netherlands (or translated from Dutch into English) are academic, business or technical works designed primarily for the specialist. The following books, however, are easy and enjoyable to read. This list is in random order:

*Living and Working in the Netherlands*. KPMG International Business Support (Amstelveen) and Formula Two Relocations (Amsterdam), 1996.

*Michelin Guides: Netherlands*. Michelin Tyre, Tourism Department, Watford (Herts), 1995.

*A Short History of the Netherlands*. Prof. de. P.J.A.N. Rietbergen and Drs. G.H.J. Seegers (translated by M.E. Bennett), Bekking Publishers, Amersfoort, 1992.

*The Xenophobe's Guide to the Dutch*. Rodney Bolt, Ravette Books, Horsham (West Sussex), 1995.

*The UnDutchables*. Colin White and Laurie Boucke, published by the authors at Montrose (California), 1991.

*The Netherlands in Brief*. Foreign Information Service, Ministry of Foreign Affairs, The Hague, 1994.

*The Low Sky*. Han Van Der Horst (translated by Andy Brown), Scriptum Books/Nuffic, The Hague, 1996.

*The Embarrassment of Riches*. Simon Schama, Fontana/Collins, 1987.

*Living & Working in the Netherlands*. Pat Rush, How To Books, Plymouth, 1996.

*Act Normal!* Hans Kaldenbach, Prometheus, Amsterdam, 1995.

*The Low Countries: Arts and Society in Flanders and the Netherlands.* A yearbook published annually by the Flemish-Netherlands Foundation "Stichting Ons Erfdeel," Flanders, Belgium.

*The Dutch Connection.* Frank E. Huggett, Netherlands Government Printing Office, The Hague, 1982.

*Spectrum of the Netherlands.* Photographs by Ursula Pfistermeister and others, Spectrum, Utrecht-Antwerp, 1985.

*Flying Over Holland.* Fred Racké (editor), aerial photographs by Aerophoto Schiphol/Aviafoto Utrecht, Promotion Pictures, Kortenhoef, 1981.

*History of the Netherlands.* Netherlands Institute for the Development and Support of Educational Projects, Maastricht, 1995.

*Practical Guide for New Residents.* Rotterdam City Development Corporation, 1996. (A free booklet which is updated every six months.)

*Foreign nationals working in the Netherlands.* Coopers & Lybrand, Amsterdam, 1997.

*Going to School in the Netherlands.* DOP, The Hague, c. 1996.

# THE AUTHOR

Hunt Janin is an American writer living in southwestern France. He has written one other book for Times Editions (*Cultures of the World: Saudi Arabia*) and two books for an American publisher *(The India-China Opium Trade in the Nineteenth Century* and *Fort Bridger, Wyoming)*. He is now working on two new books—one on the role of the Dutch West India Company in 17th century slave trade; the other on pilgrimages to Jerusalem in the last two millennia.

He has an MA in political science from the University of California (Berkeley) and was a Fellow at Harvard University and a Tutor at the Civil Service College in London. He was briefly a US Marine and a naval historian and then for 25 years he was an American diplomat, serving in India, Ghana, Lebanon, Saudi Arabia and Nepal. He is married to Corinne Janin-Nuis, a former member of the Netherlands Foreign Service. Thanks to her, he has many Dutch friends and visits the Netherlands frequently.

# INDEX